Lucy Leffingwell Cable Biklé, George Washington Cable

The Cable story book

Selections for school reading

Lucy Leffingwell Cable Biklé, George Washington Cable

The Cable story book
Selections for school reading

ISBN/EAN: 9783337275563

Printed in Europe, USA, Canada, Australia, Japan

Cover: Foto ©Andreas Hilbeck / pixelio.de

More available books at **www.hansebooks.com**

THE CABLE STORY BOOK

SELECTIONS FOR SCHOOL READING

EDITED BY

MARY E. BURT

AUTHOR OF "LITERARY LANDMARKS" AND EDITOR OF
"THE EUGENE FIELD BOOK," ETC.

AND

LUCY LEFFINGWELL CABLE

NEW YORK

CHARLES SCRIBNER'S SONS

1899

TROW DIRECTORY
PRINTING AND BOOKBINDING COMPANY
NEW YORK

PREFACE

THE CABLE STORY BOOK has been prepared
in response to a revival of interest in Mr.
Cable's works among his early admirers, as
well as to the newly awakened enthusiasm of
a younger audience and the urgent demand
from various sources for selections from his
books for school-readers.

Southern life and Southern history have never heretofore been well represented in school
reading. The Adirondacks, the Catskills,
and the Hudson have become enchanted regions to school students through the works
of Washington Irving, John Burroughs, and
Charles Dudley Warner. Hawthorne has
created an American Wonderland in New
England. Longfellow has brought Grand Pré
and all Acadia into the schoolroom through
Evangeline, and he has interpreted Indian life
to us through Hiawatha; but the great balmy
South, with its "endless colonnades of cypresses,—long motionless drapings of gray

moss,—and constellations of water-lilies," has been a matter of dry geographical statistics, and not the land of song. To read Cable is to live in the South, to bask in its sunshine, eat of its figs and pomegranates, and dream its dreams. No other writer has so recorded its pulse-beats. This book comes to fill a great gap, to furnish the interpretation of a wide district of our country before unrepresented in our schools. For these reasons the stories are pre-eminently profitable school reading.

Then, Cable's way of placing what is vital in character before the child's mind (I might better say the child's heart), at the same time that he bends down the boughs of the magnolia or orange-tree to regale him with its sweet odors, is transcendent. The child breathes in the very atmosphere of the South, but, what is of more significance, he breathes in the virtue and nobility of the writer. In no case have I ever edited a book for schools where I have felt more deeply the importance of the work. It has been a matter of the most enthusiastic pride with me. This book is one that I love. A country is sweet and beautiful and worthy of our patriotic devotion only as far as it is the home of noble souls. Those of our writers who have portrayed its natural beauty and illuminated what is heroic in its commonplaces, in a way to endear the very ground to our feet, deserve the first recognition in our schools.

The stories in this book, and many more from Mr. Cable's pen, have been read and re-read with several classes of pupils from eight to fifteen years of age ; and their reception has influenced both the choice and the arrangement of the selections, the easiest reading being placed first. The stories were received with an interest so genuine that requests were often pressed urgently to "go on with the story" instead of the regular lesson. In using these stories many interesting incidents have occurred. Only yesterday I picked up a picture from the floor which a little boy had drawn to illustrate the fire in the story "The Taxidermist." An excited crowd was represented standing around the fire, and "me at this fire" was printed under the most excited individual there. The stream of water was larger than the house. Mr. Cable is notedly delicate in his composition, and it might be a matter of conjecture whether an author so exclusive and cultured would be comprehended by the children. But I have only to refer to their little written reviews to be reassured on this point. A boy of ten writes: "The Taxidermist tried to put the soul back into the little humming-bird." An older boy writes: "You would think that such a big hand could not handle such a tender animal very well." Yet another child says: "He made nice work because he was sorry the little bird was dead, and he wanted to bring the life back to the bird." A boy less than ten years old writes: "I think Jean-ah Poquelin was very brave to hide his brother and take care of him when he had the leprosy, for he might have taken it himself." Bras Coupé, too, is a hero close to the heart of children. His roar of delight on seeing his bride-elect at his wedding always called out a responsive roar of laughter, and his capture with the lasso a sigh of pity. His disdain of slaveship found willing endorsement, for children are really freemen. And there is not any temperance tale more suitably adapted to the necessities of responsive reading than "Gregory's Island." Hawthorne says: "Children possess an unestimated sensibility to whatever is deep or high in imagination or feeling so long as it is simple, likewise. It is only the artificial and complex that bewilder them."

I have spoken only of the needs of the schools of our own country; but I have often observed in book-stores and at book-stalls in

England and Scotland that of the few American writers who receive acknowledgment there, Mr. Cable's books always stand side by side with Hawthorne's, Longfellow's, Burroughs', and Howells'. As I travelled through those countries last summer, wherever I went I met constant mention and praise of Mr. Cable's stories as he had read them among all classes.

The difficulty of Mr. Cable's English has in former years kept him out of the schoolroom. This "difficulty" has consisted partly in the dialect of his stories and partly in his extreme luxuriance of detail in descriptions. To understand Mr. Cable one must approach him as one would Tennyson or Lowell, by taking those studies first which furnish a key to his habitual attitude of mind and manner of thought. Once in possession of this clew, one finds himself on the author's own territory, and "the difficulty of his English" disappears. In editing this volume, only such changes have been made as seemed advisable to make it a key to all of Mr. Cable's writings, not only for young people, but for the general public. No liberties have been taken with the text, except with Mr. Cable's approval; no changes made that were not necessary to render the reading perfectly easy to a very young audience.

Where the children have asked for explanations, there the changes have been made. It is the author's own statement that it has often occurred to him to prepare such a key as this to his works for the reading public, and in fact I have the pleasure of acknowledging Mr. Cable's collaboration in an appreciable degree.

I linger with grateful affection over these pages. My only regret is that "The Taxidermist," of which the children were so fond, found no room in the book, and that several other valuable schoolroom stories could not be included.

MARY E. BURT.

THE JOHN A. BROWNING SCHOOL,
    NEW YORK, March 4, 1899.

CONTENTS

ILLUSTRATIONS

THE CABLE STORY BOOK

THE CHILDREN'S NEW ORLEANS

MOST of those who go to New Orleans in these days of haste reach it by rail. If they come through Mississippi or Alabama, they run for a long time through a rolling country, wild in a most gentle way, and covered with towering pines in almost unbroken forests.

Then they come to flat lands. They cross pine-barrens, sea-marshes, quaking prairies, and tangled swamps of gum trees and dwarf palmetto, or of cypress—the lofty kind that is not evergreen. These great cypresses, with their perpetual drapery of Spanish moss (often eight feet long), are very dreary in winter. But they are solemnly beautiful in the eight months of spring's green and of summer's purple haze and golden glow.

Or on some warm spring day, with Mobile at his back, the traveller comes out upon the low shores of Mississippi Sound, at the great delta's eastern corner, and spins out across

Grand Plains, that are robed in green rushes, belted by the blue sky and bluer gulf, garlanded like a May-queen with mallows, morning-glories, and the flower-de-luce, and clad in the steel and silver of salty lakelets and ponds.

But those who come from these directions meet one drawback: they must enter the town through its back yard, so to speak. But presently the river-front is reached—the levee, the sugar-sheds, the shipping, the long steamboat-landing. Here the city's commercial life is before you, and you leave the train at the foot of Canal Street, the apple of New Orleans' eye.

Some visitors to the city approach it by steamboat, coming down the Mississippi River. These, by the time they arrive, are familiar with sugar-plantations, negro-quarters, planters' homes, islands of willow and cottonwood, and the fascinating hurly-burly of the steamboat's lower deck, where the black roustabouts laugh and sing while performing prodigious labors.

Others, but they are a very few, arrive by ocean-steamer, through the world-renowned Eads jetties, parallel piers of wood and stone, narrowing the mouth of the river like the nozzle on a hose, to make the current swift and deep. These visitors have to ascend the river's hundred or so miles where it runs below the city, eastward—not south—to empty for all time its myriad tons of red and yellow Rocky Mountain sand into that ever quaking sieve, the wonderful blue waters of the Gulf of Mexico.

These travellers by the great steamers have seen no end of rice-fields and sugar-houses, groves of orange, and plantation avenues of live-oak and pecan trees. They have come by Forts Jackson and St. Philip, which Farragut, on that ever famous April night in 1862, ran past with his wooden ships while the thundering forts were trying to make remains of him. And they have come round English Turn, a bend in the river where Bienville, the founder of New Orleans and "Father of Louisiana," once met some English explorers, and induced them to turn back by telling them something very much like a fib: English Turn, where, nearly a century and a half later, the frenzied people of New Orleans first saw the masts and yards of Farragut's fleet, and the flash of his guns as he silenced the last battery between him and them. And lastly, they have steamed by the old battle-ground where, on the 8th of January, 1815, Andrew Jackson and his Kentuckians, Tennesseeans, and Louisiana Creoles, all Indian-fighters and bear and deer hunters, taught the military world the value of straight aiming and sharp-shooting. If you should ever be leaving New Orleans for the North, no route is so delightful as this one, down the river, across toward Havana, through the Straits of Florida, and up the Gulf Stream.

My first visit to New Orleans was by none of these ways: I arrived there for the first time on the occasion of my birth. I have it from members of my family that I came up through the ground from China. However that may be, I could hardly have looked around—when I learned how to do so—without being interested in my neighborhood. The house's garden and grounds were bounded four-square by an unbroken line—a hedge, almost—of orange-trees, in which the orchard-oriole sang by day and the mocking-bird all night. Along the garden walks grew the low, drooping trees of that kindest—to good children—of all tree-fruits, the fig; though many's the time and many's the fig-tree in which I've made my mouth sore—so sore I couldn't laugh with comfort—through eating the fig, by the dozen dozen, with its skin on, rather than lose three seconds to peel it. Even when time isn't money, often it's figs.

THE HOUSE ON ANNUNCIATION SQUARE, NEW ORLEANS, IN WHICH MR. CABLE WAS BORN.

In later years, when the history of this region became as true a delight to me as its fruits, I learned that Louisiana owes the orange and the fig to a company of French Jesuit Fathers who brought them to New Orleans very soon after the city itself was born, and while it was still a tiny, puny thing of mere cabins, green with weeds and willows, and infested with musk-rats, mosquitos, snakes, frogs, and alligators.

The house of which I speak stood, and still stands, without any special history of its own, on a very small fraction of the lands given to those priests by the French king. In front of it is Annunciation Square, from whose northern gate one looked down a street of the same name.

From New Orleans' earliest days, Annunciation Street was a country road, fronted along its western side by large colonial villas standing in their orangeries and fig-orchards, and looking eastward, from their big windows, across the Mississippi River. Though they stood well back from the river-bank, they were whole squares nearer it than they are, or would be, now: the river has moved off sidewise. Ever since the city's beginnings, the muddy current has been dumping sand and making land along that whole front. Now, instead of

the planter's carriage toiling through the mire,
one meets, in granite-paved Annunciation
Street, and others to the east of it, the cotton-
float with its three- or four-mule team and its
lofty load of bales going to or from the " com-
press." For it is the cotton-compress whose
white cloud of steam and long, gasping roar
break at frequent intervals upon the air, signi-
fying, each time, that one more bale of the
beautiful fleece has been squeezed in an instant
to a fourth of its former bulk, and is ready to
be shipped to New or Old England, to France
or Russia, for the world's better comfort or
delight. I could tell you of a certain man who,
when a boy, used to waste hours watching the
negro "gangs" as, singing lustily and reeking
to their naked waists, they pressed bale after
bale under the vast machinery. Yes, he would
be glad to waste an hour or two more in the
same way with you, even now, when time
has come to be infinitely more than either figs
or money. Don't miss the weird, inspiring
scene, if ever you go to New Orleans.

Moving down Annunciation Street from the
square, something like a mile away one reaches
not its end but its beginning; for here it comes
toward us out of another and much more noted
thoroughfare, whose roadway ever swarms—

Sundays and dog-days excepted—with floats and drays. Even street-cars often have to beg their way by littles, and its noisy sidewalks are choked with the transit of boxes, crates, and barrels of the city's wholesale trade in things wet and dry for the table, the sideboard, and the luncheon-basket. For this is Tchoupitoulas Street. You may call it Choop-e-too-lah.

As Annunciation Street leaves it, it dives in among cotton-presses, junk-shops, and tobacco-warehouses, and comes out among ship-wharves, storehouses of salt and of ice, piles of lumber, staves, and shingles, wood-yards, flat-boat-landings, fleets of coal-barges, sawmills, truck-gardens, and brick-kilns, and at length, miles away, escapes into the country and up the great bends of the ever-winding river. It was once the road to and through the village of the Tchoupitoulas subtribe of Indians, the town's first and nearest human neighbors. You may call them Choop-e-too-lah, also. It starts nearly at a right angle from the river end of Canal Street, now the fairest and most popular avenue of New Orleans.

We have come to Canal Street no sooner than everyone does who visits New Orleans at all. One seeks it as naturally as he seeks the eye of a person to whom he would speak.

Canal Street is the city's optic nerve. Upon
Canal Street all processions and pageants—a
delightsome word to New Orleans ears—make
their supreme display. Any street-car you
find will sooner or later bring you to Canal
Street, if you should ever get lost in a town so
level, long, and narrow that you are never for
five minutes out of sight of the masts in the
harbor. Here are the largest and finest retail
stores of the kinds our mothers and sisters love
to haunt; here are the chief cake and candy
shops, too. From here the cars start which
carry their thousands of people on heated afternoons to the waterside resorts of Lake Pontchartrain, some four or six miles away north-
ward; and here is the dividing line between
the New Orleans of the English-speaking
American and that of the French-speaking
Creole.

Like all the cross-streets of the " Crescent
City," Canal Street sleeps with the levee for
its pillow. I mean the land is lower than the
river when the waters are up, and the levee is
an embankment along the river's margin,
thrown up to keep the Mississippi in its own
bed and let New Orleans sleep peacefully on
hers.

What enormous quantities of freight are

here, in rows and piles! Bales, barrels, and casks, with or without canvas covers to shield them from the rain of sunbeams even more than of water-drops. Scores of little flags of many colors and devices flutter over them. These are to enable the negroes who unload the boats to sort their burdens as directed by the stevedore, who stands at the gang-plank to see the mark of each package as it comes by him, and give its bearer or bearers his order accordingly.

"Go to de blue flag! Go to de red an' yalleh! Go to de white cross! Go to de check flag! Go to de blue anchor! Go to de check an' green!"

It is fascinating to watch, from the upper decks of some great packet-boat, this distribution of huge treasure by the hands of these ragged black Samsons. Sometimes the orders sound like curses.

"Go to de red hand! Go to de black heart! Go to de green moon! Go to de black flag!"

This levee was once a battle-field. That was years ago, though since the great civil war. There was a real battle, with infantry and artillery, and many were killed and wounded, and a State government changed hands as a result of it; but though men are quite willing to tell you of it if you ask, not even those who won the battle say much about it without being asked, now ; for it was that worst of all kinds of fighting, called civil strife, and the levee offers many pleasanter themes.

When the afternoon hour is nearly five, as the lofty steamers' deep-toned bells begin to toll, and their towering funnels pour forth torrent clouds of black smoke, hundreds of people gather along the levee's front to see the majestic departures of the vast yet graceful crafts. One after another, with flags and pennants streaming, they back out from the landing, turning their bows up-stream, fall away for a few moments before the mighty current of a river one hundred feet deep, then stand still against it, and the next moment spring forward with a peal from their parting gun and the down-run of all their flags, and speed away, while the black deck-hands, in a crowd about the great front mast, called the jack-staff, sing defiance to weariness and fate. All along the city's front for miles, as they pass, men and boys pull out in skiffs to " take the waves" which rise behind their great paddle-wheels; for a Mississippi River side-wheeler " tears the river wide open," as they say. In the warm months many fellows swim out in-

stead of rowing ; but, believe me, the "Father
of Waters" is dangerous enough even for a
skiff ; it is no fit place for a swimmer.

This description applies mainly to the "upper
levee"—that is, the part above Canal Street.
The lower has other features. It begins at
Canal Street with the "lower steamboat land-
ing." Here, about and under the sugar-sheds, the
State's great sugar and molasses crop is handled.

Near the French market, beyond, lie the
steamships that run to New York. And here
is that picturesque scene, the Picayune Tier,
where the Spaniards' and Sicilians' luggers,
many of them with red sails, huddle together,
unloading across one another's half-decks their
cargoes of oysters, melons, garlics, egg-plants,
sweet-peppers, pecans, and oranges. Just beyond it begins the long crescent of the "lower
shipping," both steam and sail. Much of this
is from Liverpool, Havre, or Hamburg, coming after cotton, cotton, cotton ; but much,
too—brigs, barks, ships, with hulls white, blue,
or green—is from the Mediterranean, the Penin-
sula, "the Bay of Biscay, O," and the Antilles,
bringing lemons, olives, almonds, prunes, wines,
cordials, raisins, sardines, cocoanuts, bananas,
coffee, cacao, dates, and cinnamon, yet never
uttering one single "Have some?" to the boys

who stand about with flattened stomachs and watering mouths. There! that boy's got a banana!—Catch him!—Who?—He's a half-mile away, and still going; earning his banana by the sweat of his legs.

Let us turn back to the French market. For there is beautiful, quaint old Jackson Square, and behind it the twin spires of St. Louis Cathedral, both of them just where Bienville staked out the ground for them a hundred and seventy-five years ago. He called the square (and it was so called for more than a century) the Place d'Armes. The plan was for six streets to run behind the square, parallel with the river-bank, with six crossing them at right angles on the square's left, and six others doing the same on its right, the whole having the levee in front and a wall of earth and palisades on the other three sides. Certain streets even yet show by their names where this old wall and its moat were—Canal Street, Rampart, Esplanade—making what is still called the old square. This is but a slender fraction of the present Creole New Orleans below Canal Street; but it is the old, the historic Creole Quarter; and there was not much more than this even when Claiborne, the young Virginian, was the first governor of the State of Louisiana, and Andrew Jackson, the saviour of New Orleans, parleyed, in yonder room whose windows still look out upon the old square, with Lafitte, the pirate of the Gulf of México, and accepted his aid to drive back the British invader. Now the long, thin city stretches up and down the bends of its river-harbor twelve miles and more, and promises ere long to have a quarter of a million inhabitants.

Just behind the old square, and facing Rampart Street midway between Canal and Esplanade, just as Jackson Square faces the levee, is a piece of public ground "whose present name of Congo Square," as somebody says, "still preserves a reminder of its old barbaric pastimes." For here is where the Creoles' slaves, when this was outside the town gates, used to dance their wild dances, the Bamboula and Calinda. Here, for many years, was a famous circus and many a bull-fight. Here is where Parson Jones preached, and where Bras Coupé was lassoed. You do not know them? It doesn't matter; they were only friends of mine; but I hope you will know them sometime, when you are grown older.

Children love New Orleans!
I have seen a great many large cities, but I

cannot think I have ever seen one so green with trees or so full of song-birds and flowers. All summer the magnolia opens its large, white, delicate blossoms of ravishing fragrance among its glossy leaves so high in air that only a stout-hearted boy can climb up and pick them. When its bursting seed-cones drop to the pavement and scatter their shining coral seeds, little girls with needle and thread string these seeds into necklaces whose perfume is even finer than that of the flowers. I do not say they always smell the sweet odor; some little girls have such small noses!

We must not stop to tell of half the flowers. We may not dwell even upon the orange-blossoms. Yet there is one of Flora's lesser gems which we must not leave untold. It is the children's flower — the frail, sweet-scented little red, white, and yellow trumpets of the "four-o'clock." The little girls of New Orleans string many thousand garlands of these blossoms in a single summer afternoon. And then there is the china-tree, whose large bunches of tiny purple flowers the girls cannot get unless the boys climb the trees, break off the sprays, and drop them down. Some boys—even some very respectable boys—prefer not to do this! Later in the year they climb the same trees and fill their pockets with the green china-berries, which make the best wads you ever saw, for popguns. These, fortunately, last but a short while, whereas there is no time of year in New Orleans when one may not gather roses and violets in the open air, and without having to ask the boys for them.

Oh, yes, children have good reason to love New Orleans. Its climate, the doctors say, is kind to babies. It is true, one can never go sleighing there, and a day of good snowballing comes only about once in ten years; but then neither can one get his ears or toes frozen, except by going to one of the big ice-factories and paying to have it done.

The nature of the soil, too, has advantages and attractions. Almost everywhere except along the river-bank it is a tough dark-blue clay. In old times men used to build mud-houses of it, mixing Spanish moss through it as plasterers mix hair in their plaster. An excellent soft red brick is made of it in vast quantities in the very picturesque brick-yards along the river. This soil, moreover, makes the best mud-pies I have ever seen; while, rubbed on the clothes of a bright boy, it can be made to procure him more old-fashioned family thrashings than any other mud I know of.

This brings us naturally to the subject of fishing. The New Orleans boy rarely fishes in the Mississippi. "Pot-fishers," that is men who fish for a living, catch its ugly buffalo-fish, and the huge fish of three, four, and five feet length named "blue-cats" and "mud-cats." They catch them with what they call trot-lines, long heavy lines like clothes-lines, hanging under the water, with small short lines hanging from them like stockings from the clothes-lines. The kind of boys known as "wharf-rats" have some luck with the hand-line at the edges of wharves; but as for fishing with the pole for small fry—I'll tell you.

I once saw a boy tie a railroad spike to forty feet of small line and cast the iron into the river from the stern of a steamboat lying at a wharf for repairs. That swirling, boiling current floated the spike! Imagine dropping into those waters without a line and with one's clothes and shoes on!

But that is what a great many persons, some dear little children among them, had to do one winter morning—I think it was a New Year's day—when five of those great steamboats burned to the water's edge in a few minutes, like so much straw or shavings. Some were saved by men in skiffs, while others were never seen again.

I know a man who, when a youth, saw that whole river-harbor one day dotted with drifting steamboats and ships, burning and sinking; but that was during the civil war, as the old black women who sell pies and "stage-planks" (gingerbread) on the landings would tell you.

No, the right sort of New Orleans boy fishes in Lake Pontchartrain—when he can afford it —and sometimes catches that handsome and delicious pan-fish, the croaker, and even the sheepshead. They are so named because the croaker makes a little croaking noise as he flounces about in your fishing-boat, and the sheepshead has a face whose profile is like that of a sheep's, and some true teeth that show with his mouth shut, like your Aunt Maria's.

The lake is five or six miles from the main streets of the city, and is thirty miles wide and over forty long, so that as one looks across it he sees only sky and water meet and vessels sink below or rise above the blue horizon.

Away back in the geological ages, before anybody's aunt was born, the Mississippi River used to run through this lake.

But New Orleans boys have other fishing-grounds. With one's father or uncle along,

2

Harvey's Canal, the Company Canal, Lake Sal-
vador, are good, better, best.   On a pinch, there
are plenty of fun and quite enough fish still
nearer by; for in all the suburban regions.
where the live-oaks spread their brawny, moss-
draped arms, or the persimmon drops its yellow fruit, the plain is crisscrossed with drain-
ing-ditches of all sizes, most of them untainted
by sewage.

And in their sometimes clear, sometimes tur-
bid waters are the sun-perch, the warmouth,
and other good fish.   Even for girls—who,
somehow, can't learn to catch real fish, poor
things!—there is in these harmless waters the
loveliest crawfishing.

I once knew a boy to catch five pretty sun-
perch in one of these big ditches, pack them
alive in some fresh Spanish moss well wetted,
put them into a covered tin bucket, carry them
three miles in the hot summer weather, turn
them into a tiny pond at his home, and keep
them there—I forget how long, but for more
than a year.   They lived upon, and gradually
exterminated, a minute species of shell-fish
which the same boy had earlier introduced,
and which from two or three specimens had
increased to thousands.

One pretty fact about the sun-perch is that

he gets married. Yes, these fish have mates, as birds do. They even have a simple sort of sandy nest. One of the pleasantest things I ever observed in all my boyhood was one of these beautiful little creatures hovering over a bright spot in the clean sand at the bottom of some cool, shallow water, the tiny hollow which was its nest, fanning it with its gauzy fins, whirling, backing, darting, and guarding it against all enemies.

But that really has nothing to do with New Orleans, except that our wandering into it thus only tends to show, I think, how very near to dear Mother Nature New Orleans is, for a city: especially the children's part of it. I was near forgetting to say that there are also snakes in those ditches: one must be candid. But they are — what shall we say? — diffident and retiring.

Even when one of them pokes his tongue out at you, that only means : " Hello, sonny, I used to know your grandma!" If, when you are fishing, you jerk up your line, thinking you have got a fish, and you find it's nothing but a mere four-foot snake, all you have to do is to drop everything and walk away rapidly. Still it is well to notice where you step. Snakes, too, go in pairs, and you don't want to tread on one snake while walking away from another. Many people consider it a sign of bad luck. Understand me, a Louisiana boy never *runs* from a snake.

One day a boy who made it a rule never to part company with a snake till he had killed it, seeing a large snake near the New Shell Road, and keeping his eyes on him sharply while he stooped to take up a stick, grasped, instead, another snake! Both these snakes got away, and the same may be said of the boy. Some of the lads of my acquaintance used to have a bad trick of catching a live snake by the tail, twirling him around as one would twirl a sling, and popping his head off as we pop a whip. The fact of the snake being venomous did not deter the boy or save the serpent. But this sport, while injurious to the snake, is not morally helpful to the boy, and I do not recommend it. I could name many other amusements, common in New Orleans, of which boys in Northern towns seem to know but little. For instance, I have never seen blow-guns outside of that city. These are sold by Choctaw Indians, mostly at the market-houses. The butchers, hucksters, fruiterers, and bakers of New Orleans, you must understand, are almost all gathered into market - houses distributed at convenient —

sometimes not too convenient—points throughout the city; and people with market-baskets
on their arms throng the gas-lighted aisles of
these long depots of supply at very early morning hours.

Any early-rising New Orleans boy or girl
will promise to be good, if father or mother
will take him or her along when going to market before breakfast. There is always a delightful uproar in these places in the hour of
dawn; a bewildering chatter of all the world
talking at once, mostly in German and French:
a calling and hallooing, a pounding of cleavers,
a smell of raw meat, of parsley and potatoes, of
fish, onions, pineapples, garlics, oranges, shrimp
and crabs, of hot loaves, coffee, milk, sausages
and curds, a rattling of tins, a whetting of
knives, a sawing of bones, a whistling of opera
airs, a singing of the folk-songs of Gascony and
Italia, a flutter of fowls, prattling and guffawing
of negroes, mules braying, carts rumbling—it
is great fun!

Most of these market-houses have some part
of their flagged floor left without roof; and
here, in pathetic contrast with all this hurry
and noise, one may almost always find, squat-
ted on the flags among the baskets of their own
weaving, a few Indian women and children:

gentle, silent, grave, bareheaded, barefooted, and smelling sweet of the bay-leaves, sassafras root and medicinal herbs they pile before them for sale.

If there are men with them, they are likely to offer for your purchase blow-guns. A blow-gun is six feet of hollow cane, the joints burnt out smooth with the red-hot end of a rod of iron wire. Its arrow, a foot long, is very slender, headless, and feathered with cotton lint, and is blown through the gun by the breath. They say Audubon, the great writer about birds, who was a native of New Orleans, used to get some of his smallest birds by means of a blow-gun. I am not sure I get that sentence logically correct: I suppose the birds were not his till he had got them; but any enterprising boy will see what I mean.

I am told that of late years the popularity of the blow-gun has been largely transferred to that fiendish thing made of a forked stick and a rubber strap, so terrifying to grandmothers and so justly denounced by big sisters, and sometimes called a bean-shooter, but known in New Orleans by the dreadful name of nigger-shooter. I hope I have been misinformed.

The cane furnishes another plaything. If all the rain that falls in New Orleans within a year were to fall in one big shower and not run off as it fell, it would cover the whole ground to the depth of more than five feet. Even as it is, the rains come down so quickly and run off so slowly, that one may often see many of the granite-paved streets in the heart of the city overflowed by an hour's rain, so that the sidewalks will be several inches under water.

You may wonder how, in such cases, the floods are prevented from overflowing cellars, but this is done by the following simple device: They don't have any cellars. Neither were there any underground sewers in the city until lately, for carrying off this rain-water. It runs off by open gutters, one at every sidewalk's outer edge. And so there is almost always some water in sight, clean or unclean, in whatever street one may be.

Now, with a simple thick joint-length of cane for a cylinder, open at one end and the joint at the other end pierced by a small vent-hole, and with a stick for a plunger, a soft rag neatly wrapped round one end of the plunger to give suction, you have a syringe, or "squirt," that will throw a stream of water upon a cat or dog, or a playmate's trousers, as much as forty feet away. A singular thing about this home-made toy is that its owner always thinks he can sit on the street curbstone and squirt it with frantic enthusiasm for an hour without getting his own clothes wet, though he always fails.

Throwing the lasso used to be a favorite sport in New Orleans. Those boys who were without lassos took the part of wild cattle, to add to the fun. Boys sometimes acquired great skill in the use of the lariat.

"Noyaus" (pronounced No-yo's) is a game whose charms ought to be known beyond New Orleans. Noyaus, you understand, are peach-stones : fully half the terms of the playground, in New Orleans, are French. Noyaus is played by standing at a line drawn on the ground, called a taw, and trying to toss the peach-stones into a hole in the ground close against some fence or wall. The game calls for skill and is interesting. The noyaus that fall outside the hole must be flipped in with thumb and forefinger.

The boys of New Orleans are great trappers of song-birds. During several months of the long, summery year they take thousands of orchard-orioles, cardinals, indigo-birds, and the little " painted bunting," which they call the "pop" or " pape," the pope. They catch them in trap-cages.

This trapping of birds is cruel play and very

one-sided, for a large proportion of the poor little prisoners die. If fellows must get their sport out of things that fly, why don't they find it in things that need their help to fly, as birds certainly do not?

There, for instance, are kites. But the lads of New Orleans can truly reply that this beautiful and harmless pastime is nowhere else in all our country so widely resorted to as in their city. I have seen more kites in the air on one day in New Orleans than in seven years anywhere else.

A far finer phase of the sport is the flying of kites of great size. And still another is the flying of lantern-kites by night. When it is real kite-time one may often see half a dozen of these phantom lanterns moving about in the soft summer-night air, and the kite, thread, and tail are entirely invisible.

This is all I need say about New Orleans, but I trust you may some day have the chance to go and see the place for yourself. Then a lovely light from the crescents of the Delta City shall linger in the firmament of your memory long after the suns of your childhood and youth have set, as, gently resting under the twinkling sky of aged years, you count the shooting-stars of happy recollections.

THE STORY OF BRAS-COUPÉ *

BRAS-COUPÉ, they said, had been, in Africa and under another name, a prince among his people. In a certain war he was captured, stripped of his royalty, marched down upon the beach of the Atlantic, and, attired as a true son of Adam, was sold as a slave. Passing out of first hands in exchange for a looking-glass, he was shipped in good order on board the schooner Egalité, whereof Blank was master, to be delivered without delay at the port of New Orleans.

Of the voyage little is recorded—here below; the less the better. Part of the living merchandise failed to keep; the weather was rough, the cargo large, the vessel small. However, the captain discovered there was room over the side, and there, from time to time during the voyage, he tossed the unmerchantable.

* Bras-Coupé is pronounced Brah-Coopay, with *pay* very short, not as in the word *pay*, but as if it were the first syllable of paper. Grand-is-sime is pronounced in three syllables.

Yet, when the reopened hatches let in the sweet smell of the land, Bras-Coupé had come to the upper—the buttered side of the world; the anchor slid with a rumble of relief down through the muddy fathoms of the Mississippi, and the prince could hear through the schooner's side the savage current of the river, leaping and licking about the bows, and whimpering welcomes home. A splendid picture to the eyes of the royal captive, as his head came up out of the hatchway, was the little Franco-Spanish-American city that lay on the low, brimming bank. There were little forts that showed their whitewashed teeth; there was a green parade-ground, and yellow barracks, and hospital, and cavalry stables, and custom-house, and a most inviting jail, convenient to the cathedral—all of dazzling white and yellow, with a black stripe marking the track of the great fire of 1794.

And here and there among the low roofs a lofty one with round-topped dormer windows and a breezy belvidere (or railed platform) looking out upon the plantations of coffee and indigo beyond the town.

When Bras-Coupé staggered ashore he stood but a moment among a drove of other negroes before he was sold. Agricola Fusilier, the business manager of the Grandissime estate, was so struck with admiration for the physical beauties of the chieftain that he bought the lot. Then he turned and sold him again on the spot to the owner of the plantation adjoining the Grandissimes'; that is, to Don José Martinez.

Down in the rich parish just below the city lay this plantation, known before Bras-Coupé passed away, as La Renaissance. Here it was that he entered at once upon a chapter of agreeable surprises. He was humanely met, presented with a clean garment, lifted into a cart drawn by oxen, taken to a whitewashed cabin of logs, finer than his palace at home, and made to comprehend that it was a free gift. He was also given some clean food, whereupon he fell sick. At home it would have been the part of piety for the magnate next the throne to launch him heavenward at once; but now healing doses were given him, and to his amazement he recovered. It reminded him that he was no longer king.

His name, he replied to an inquiry touching that subject, was —— ——, something in the Jaloff tongue, which he by and by condescended to render into Congo: Mioko-Koanga, in French Bras-Coupé, the Arm Cut Off. Truly it would have been easy to admit that his tribe, in losing him, had lost its strong right arm close off at the shoulder ; not so easy that the arm which might no longer shake the spear or swing the wooden sword, was no better than a useless stump never to be lifted for aught else. But whether easy to admit or not, that was his meaning.   He made himself a type of all Slavery, turning into flesh and blood the truth that all Slavery is maiming.

He beheld more luxury in a week than all his subjects had seen in a century.   Here Congo girls were dressed in cottons and flannels, worth, where he came from, an elephant's tusk apiece. Everybody wore clothes—children and lads alone excepted. Not a lion had invaded the settlement since his coming. The serpents were as nothing ; an occasional one coming up through the floor — that was all. . . .

When one day he had come to be quite himself, he was invited out into the sunshine, and escorted by the driver (a sort of foreman to the overseer), went forth dimly wondering. They reached a field where some men and women were hoeing. He had seen men and women—subjects of his—labor—a little — in Africa. The driver handed him a hoe ; he examined it with silent interest—until by signs he was requested to join the pastime.

" What? "

He spoke, not with his lips, but with the recoil of his splendid frame and the ferocious expansion of his eyes. This invitation was a cataract of lightning leaping down an ink-black sky. In one instant of all pervading clearness he read his sentence—WORK.

Bras-Coupé was six feet five. With a sweep as quick as instinct the back of the hoe smote the driver full in the head. Next, the prince lifted the nearest Congo crosswise, brought thirty-two teeth together in his wildly kicking leg and cast him away as a bad morsel; then, throwing another into the branches of a willow, and a woman over his head into a draining-ditch, he made one bound for freedom, and fell to his knees, rocking from side to side under the effect of a pistol-ball from the overseer. It had struck him in the forehead, and running around the skull in search of a soft spot, tradition—which sometimes jests—says came out in despair exactly where it had entered.

It so happened that, except the overseer, the whole company were black. Why should the trivial scandal be blabbed? A plaster or two made everything even in a short time, except in the driver's case—for the driver died.

Don José, young and austere, knew nothing about agriculture and cared as much about human nature. The overseer often thought this, but never said it; he would not trust even himself with the dangerous criticism. When he ventured to reveal the foregoing incidents to the señor he laid all the blame possible upon the man whom death had removed beyond the reach of correction, and brought his account to a climax by hazarding the assertion that Bras-Coupé was an animal that could not be whipped.

"Possible?" exclaimed the master, with gentle emphasis, "how so?"

"Perhaps señor had better ride down to the quarters," replied the overseer.

It was a great sacrifice of dignity, but the master made it.

"Bring him out."

They brought him out—chains on his feet, chains on his wrists, an iron yoke on his neck. The Spanish-Creole master had often seen the bull, with his long, keen horns and blazing eye, standing in the arena; but this was as though he had come face to face with a rhinoceros.

"This man is not a Congo," he said.

"He is a Jaloff," replied the encouraged overseer. "See his fine, straight nose; moreover, he is a prince. If I whip him he will die."

The dauntless captive and fearless master stood looking into each other's eyes until each recognized in the other his peer in physical courage, and each was struck with an admiration for the other which no after difference was sufficient entirely to destroy. Had Bras-Coupé's eye quailed but once—just for one little instant—he would have got the lash; but, as it was——

"Get an interpreter," said Don José; then, more privately, "and come to an understanding. I shall require it of you."

Where might one find an interpreter—one not merely able to render a Jaloff's meaning into Creole French, or Spanish, but with such a turn for diplomacy as would bring about an "understanding" with this African buffalo? The overseer was left standing and thinking, and Clemence, who had not forgotten who threw her into the draining-ditch, cunningly passed by.

"Ah, Clemence, we want you—for an interpreter!"

"I cannot, I cannot!" said Clemence. "Get

Miché Agricole Fusilier. He can interpret any and everything!"

"Agricola Fusilier! The last man on earth to make peace."

But there seemed to be no choice, and to Agricola the overseer went. It was but a little ride to the Grandissime place.

"I, Agricola Fusilier, stand as an interpreter to a negro? H-sir!"

"But I thought you might know of some person," said the weakening applicant, rubbing his ear with his hand.

"Ah!" replied Agricola, addressing the surrounding scenery, "if I did not—who would? You may take Palmyre."

The overseer softly smote his hands together at the happy thought.

"Yes," said Agricola, "take Palmyre; she has picked up as many negro dialects as I know European languages."

And she went to the don's plantation as interpreter, followed by Agricola's prayer to Fate that she might in some way be overtaken by disaster. The two hated each other with all the strength they had. He knew not only her pride, but her love for the absent Honoré, the brother of her beloved mistress; a love as fierce and wild as Bras-Coupé's self-regard. He hated her, also, for her intelligence, for the high favor in which she stood with her mistress, and for her invincible spirit, which was more offensively patent to him than to others, since he was himself the chief object of her silent detestation.

It was Palmyre's habit to do nothing without painstaking. "When Mademoiselle is married to Don José," thought she—she knew that her mistress and the don were affianced—"it will be well to have Don José's esteem. I shall endeavor to succeed." It was from this motive, then, that with the aid of her mistress she attired herself in a resplendence of scarlet and beads and feathers that could not fail the double purpose of connecting her with the children of Ethiopia and commanding the captive's instant admiration.

Alas for those who succeed too well! No sooner did the African turn his tiger glance upon her than the fire of his eyes died out; and when she spoke to him in the dear accents of his native tongue, the matter of strife vanished from his mind. He loved.

He sat down tamely in his irons and listened to Palmyre's argument as a wrecked mariner would listen to ghostly church-bells. He would give a short assent, feast his eyes, again assent, and feast his ears; but when at length she made bold to approach the real question, and finally uttered the loathed word, *Work*, he rose up, six feet five, a statue of indignation in black marble.

And then Palmyre, too, rose up, glorying in him, and went to explain to master and overseer. Bras-Coupé understood, she said, that he was a slave—it was the fortune of war, and he was a warrior; but, according to a generally recognized principle in African international law, he could not reasonably be expected to work.

"As Señor will remember I told him," remarked the overseer; "how can a man expect to plough with a zebra?"

Here he recalled a fact in his early experience. An African of this stripe had been found to answer admirably as a "driver" to make others work. A second and third parley, extending through two or three days, were held with the prince, looking to his appointment to the vacant office of driver; yet what was the master's amazement to learn at length that his Highness declined the proffered honor.

"Stop!" spoke the overseer again, detecting a look of alarm in Palmyre's face as she turned away. "She lies, he does not decline the honor! Let me take the man to Agricola!"

"No!" cried Palmyre, with an agonized look, "I will tell. He will take the place and fill it if you will give me to him for his wife—but oh, gentlemen, for the love of God—I do not want to be his wife!"

The overseer looked at the Señor, ready to approve whatever he should decide. Bras-Coupé's intrepid audacity took the Spaniard's heart by irresistible assault.

"I leave it entirely with Señor Fusilier," he said.

"But he is not my master; he has no right to give me to anyone."

"Silence!"

And she was silent; and so, sometimes, is fire in the wall.

Agricola's consent was given with malicious promptness, and as Bras-Coupé's fetters fell off it was decreed that, should he fill his office well, there should be a wedding on the rear veranda of the Grandissime mansion at the same time with the one already appointed to take place in the grand hall of the same house six months from that present day. In the meanwhile Palmyre should remain with Mademoiselle, who had promptly but quietly made up her mind that Palmyre should not be wed unless she wished to be. Bras-Coupé made no objection, was royally worthless for a time, but learned fast, mastered the "gumbo" dialect in a few weeks, and in six months was the most valuable man ever bought for Spanish dollars. Nevertheless, there were but three persons within as many square miles who were not most vividly afraid of him.

The first was Palmyre. His bearing in her presence was ever one of solemn, exalted respect, which, whether from pure magnanimity in himself, or by reason of her magnetic eye, was something worth being there to see. "It was royal!" said the overseer.

The second was not that official. When Bras-Coupé said—as, at stated intervals, he did say—"I go to Agricola Fusilier to see my betrothed," the overseer would sooner have intercepted a score of painted Chickasaws than that one lover. He would look after him and shake a prophetic head. "Trouble coming; better not deceive that fellow;" yet that was the very thing Palmyre dared do. Her admiration for Bras-Coupé was almost boundless. She rejoiced in his stature; she revelled in the contemplation of his untamable spirit; he seemed to her the gigantic embodiment of her own dark, fierce will, the expanded realization of her life-time longing for terrible strength. But

. . . her heart she could not give him—she did not have it. Yet after her first prayer to the Spaniard and his overseer for deliverance, to the secret surprise and chagrin of her young mistress, she pretended to be contented. It was a trick; she knew Agricola's power, and to seem to consent was her one chance with him. He might thus be beguiled into withdrawing his own consent. That failing, she had Mademoiselle's promise to come to the rescue, which she could use at the last moment; and that failing, she had a dirk. . . .

The second person who did not fear Bras-Coupé was Mademoiselle. On one of the giant's earliest visits to see Palmyre he obeyed the summons which she brought him, to appear before the lady. A more artificial man might have objected on the score of dress, his attire being a single gaudy garment tightly enveloping the waist and thighs. As his eyes fell upon the beautiful white lady he prostrated himself upon the ground, his arms outstretched before him. He would not move till she was gone. Then he arose like a hermit who has seen a vision. " Bras-Coupé dares not look upon a spirit." From that hour he worshipped. He saw her often; every time, after one glance at her countenance, he would prostrate his gigantic length with his face in the dust.

The third person who did not fear him was —was it Agricola? Nay, it was the Spaniard— a man whose capability to fear anything in nature or beyond had never been discovered.

Long before the wedding-day Bras-Coupé would have slipped the entanglements of bondage, though as yet he felt them only as one feels a spider's web across the face, had not the master, according to a little affectation of the times, promoted him to be his gamekeeper. Many a day did these two living magazines of wrath spend together in the dismal swamps and on the meagre intersecting ridges, making war upon deer and bear and wildcat; or on the Mississippi after wild goose and pelican; when even a word misplaced would have made either the slayer of the other. Yet the months ran smoothly round and the wedding night drew nigh. A goodly company had assembled. All things were ready. The bride was dressed, the bridegroom had come. On the great back piazza, which had been inclosed with sail-cloth and lighted with lanterns, was Palmyre, full of a new and deep design and playing her deceit to the last, robed in costly garments to whose beauty was added the charm of their having been worn once, and once only, by her beloved Mademoiselle.

But where was Bras-Coupé?

The question was asked of Palmyre by Agricola with a gaze that meant in English, " No tricks, girl! "

Among the servants who huddled at the windows and door to see the inner magnificence a frightened whisper was already going round.

" We have made a sad discovery, Miché Fusilier," said the overseer. " Bras-Coupé is here; we have him in a room just yonder. But—the truth is, sir, Bras-Coupé is a voudou."

" Well, and suppose he is; what of it? Only hush; do not let his master know it. It is nothing; all the blacks are voudous, more or less."

" But he declines to dress himself — has painted himself all rings and stripes, antelope-fashion."

" Tell him Agricola Fusilier says, ' dress immediately! ' "

" Oh, Miché, we have said that five times already, and his answer—you will pardon me— his answer is—spitting on the ground—that you are a contemptible white trash."

There is nothing to do but to call the very

bride—the lady herself. She comes forth in all her glory, small, but oh, so beautiful! Slam! Bras-Coupé is upon his face, his finger-tips touching the tips of her snowy slippers. She gently bids him go and dress, and at once he goes.

Ah! now the question may be answered without whispering. There is Bras-Coupé, towering above all heads, in ridiculous red and blue regimentals, but with a look of savage dignity upon him that keeps everyone from laughing. The murmur of admiration that passed along the thronged gallery leaped up into a shout in the bosom of Palmyre. Oh, Bras-Coupé — heroic soul! She would not falter. She would let the silly priest say his say—then her cunning should help her *not to be* his wife, yet to show his mighty arm how and when to strike.

" He is looking for Palmyre," said some, and at that moment he saw her.

" Ho-o-o-o-o!" he roared.

Agricola's best roar was a penny trumpet to Bras-Coupé's note of joy. The whole mascu- line half of the in-door company flocked out to see what the matter was. Bras-Coupé was taking her hand in one of his and laying his other upon her head; and, as some one made an unnecessary gesture for silence, he sang, beating slow and solemn time with his naked foot and with the hand that dropped hers to smite his breast:

> " On the mountain chain, my friends,
>   I've been cutting cane, my friends,
>   Money for to gain, my friends,
>   For to give Palmyre.
>   Ah! Palmyre, Palmyre, my love, my true,
>   I love you, dear—I love, I love, love you."

"Mountain?" asked one slave of another. "What's a mountain? We haven't such things in Louisiana."

"But there are mountains a-plenty in Africa; listen!"

> " Ah! Palmyre, my little bird, Palmyre,
>   I love you, love; I love you, love you, dear."

"Bravissimo!—" but just then a counter-attraction drew the white company back into the house. An old French priest, with sandalled feet and a dirty face, had arrived. There was a moment of hand-shaking with the good father, then a moment of palpitation and holding of the breath, and then—you would have known it by the turning away of two or three feminine heads in tears—the lily hand became the don's, to have and to hold, by authority of the Church and the Spanish king. And all was merry, save that outside there was coming up as villainous a night as ever cast black looks in through snug windows.

It was just as the newly-wed Spaniard, with Agricola and all the guests, were concluding the by-play of marrying the darker couple, that the hurricane struck the dwelling. The holy and jovial father had made faint pretence of kissing this second bride; the ladies, colonels, dons, etc.—though the joke struck them as a trifle coarse—were beginning to laugh and clap hands again and the gowned jester to bow to right and left, when Bras-Coupé, tardily realizing the consummation of his hopes, stepped forward to embrace his wife.

" Bras-Coupé ! "

The voice was that of Palmyre's mistress. She had not been able to comprehend her maid's behavior, but now Palmyre had darted upon her an appealing look.

The warrior stopped as if a javelin had flashed over his head and stuck in the wall.

" Bras-Coupé must wait till I give him his wife."

He sank, with hidden face, slowly to the floor.

"Bras-Coupé hears the voice of zombis; the voice is sweet, but the words are very strong; from the same sugar-cane comes molasses and rum; Bras-Coupé says to zombis, 'Bras-Coupé will wait; but if the white trash deceive Bras-Coupé—'" he rose to his feet with his eyes closed and his great black fist lifted over his head—"Bras-Coupé will call the great god of the Voudous!"

The crowd retreated and the storm fell like a burst of infernal applause. A whiff like fifty witches flouted up the canvas curtain of the gallery, and a fierce black cloud, drawing the moon under its cloak, belched forth a stream of fire that seemed to flood the ground; a peal of thunder followed as if the sky had fallen in, the house quivered, the great oaks groaned, and every lesser thing bowed down before the awful blast. Every lip held its breath for a minute—or an hour, no one knew—there was a sudden lull of the wind, and the floods came down. Have you heard it thunder and rain in those Louisiana lowlands? Every clap seems to crack the world. It has rained a moment; you peer through the black pane—your house is an island, all the land is sea.

However, the supper was spread in the hall and in due time the guests were filled. Then

a supper was spread in the big hall in the basement, below stairs, the sons and daughters of
Ham came down like the fowls of the air upon
a rice-field, and Bras-Coupé, throwing his heels
about with the joyous carelessness of a smutted
Mercury, for the first time in his life tasted the
blood of the grape. A second, a fifth, a tenth
time he tasted it, drinking more deeply each
time, and would have taken it ten times more
had not his bride cunningly concealed it. It
was like stealing a tiger's kittens.

The moment quickly came when he wanted
his eleventh bumper. As he presented his
request a silent shiver of consternation ran
through the dark company ; and when, in what
the prince meant as a remonstrative tone, he
repeated the petition—splitting the table with
his fist by way of punctuation—there ensued a
hustling up staircases and a cramming into
dim corners that left him alone at the banquet.

Leaving the table, he strode up-stairs and
into the chirruping and dancing of the grand
salon. There was a halt in the cotillion and a
hush of amazement like the shutting off of
steam. Bras-Coupé strode straight to his
master, laid his paw upon his fellow-bride-
groom's shoulder, and, in a thunder-tone, demanded :

" More ! "

The master swore a Spanish oath, lifted his hand and—fell, beneath the terrific fist of his slave, with a bang that jingled the candelabras. Dolorous stroke!—for the dealer of it.   Given, apparently to him—poor, tipsy savage—in self-defence, punishable, in a white offender, by a small fine or a few days' imprisonment, it assured Bras-Coupé, because he was black, the death of a felon; such was the old law. . . .

The guests stood for an instant as if frozen, smitten stiff with the instant expectation of insurrection, conflagration, and rapine, while, single-handed and naked-fisted in a room full of swords, the giant stood over his master, making strange signs and passes and rolling out, in wrathful words of his mother-tongue, what it needed no interpreter to tell his swarming enemies was a voudou curse.

"We are bewitched!" screamed two or three ladies, " we are bewitched!"

" Look to your wives and daughters!" shouted a Grandissime.

"Shoot the black devils without mercy!" cried another, unconsciously putting into a single outflash of words, the whole Creole treatment of race troubles.

With a single bound, Bras-Coupé reached

the drawing-room door ; his gaudy regimentals made a red and blue streak down the hall; there was a rush of frilled and powdered gentlemen to the rear veranda, an avalanche of lightning with Bras-Coupé in the midst making for the swamp, and then all without was blackness of darkness and all within was a wild, commingled chatter of Creole, French, and Spanish tongues—in the midst of which the reluctant Agricola returned his dress-sword to its scabbard.

While the wet lanterns swung on crazily in the trees along the way by which the bridegroom was to have borne his bride, while Madame Grandissime prepared an impromptu bridal-chamber, while the Spaniard bathed his eye and the blue gash on his cheek-bone, while Palmyre paced her room in a fever and wild tremor of conflicting emotions throughout the night, and the guests splashed home after the storm as best they could, Bras-Coupé was practically declaring his independence on a slight rise of ground hardly sixty feet in circumference and lifted scarce above the water in the inmost depths of the swamp.

And amid what surroundings ! Endless colonnades of cypresses; long, motionless drapings of gray moss; broad sheets of noisome

waters, pitchy black, resting on bottomless
ooze; cypress knees studding the surface;
patches of floating green, gleaming brilliantly
here and there; yonder, where the sunbeams
wedge themselves in, constellations of water-
lilies, the many-hued iris, and a multitude of
flowers that no man had named; here, too,
serpents great and small, of wonderful color-
ings, and the dull and loathsome moccasin,
sliding warily off the dead tree; in dimmer
recesses, the cow alligator, with her nest hard
by; turtles, a century old; owls and bats, rac-
coons, opossums, rats, centipedes and creatures
of like vileness; great vines of beautiful leaf
and scarlet fruit in deadly clusters; madden-
ing mosquitoes, parasitic insects, gorgeous
dragon-flies and pretty water-lizards; the blue
heron, the snowy crane, the red-bird, the moss-
bird, the night-hawk and the whip-will's-wid-
ow; a solemn stillness and stifled air only now
and then disturbed by the call or whir of the
summer duck, the dismal note of the rain-crow,
or the splash of a dead branch falling into the
clear but lifeless bayou.

The pack of Cuban hounds that howl from
Don José's kennels cannot snuff the trail of
the stolen canoe that glides through the som-
bre blue vapors of the African's fastnesses. His

arrows send no tell-tale reverberations to the distant clearing. Many a wretch in his native wilderness has Bras-Coupé himself, in palmier days, driven to just such an existence, to escape the chains and horrors of the slave-pens; therefore, not a whit broods he over man's inhumanity, but, taking the affair as a matter of course, casts about him for a future.

Bras-Coupé let the autumn pass, and wintered in his den.

Don José, in a majestic way, endeavored to be happy. He took his Señora to his hall, and under her rule, it took on for awhile a look and feeling which turned it from a hunting-lodge into a home. Wherever the lady's steps turned—or it is as correct to say, wherever the proud tread of Palmyre turned—the features of bachelor's hall disappeared; guns, dogs, oars, saddles, nets, went their way into proper banishment, and the broad halls and lofty chambers—the floors now muffled with mats of palmetto-leaf—no longer re-echoed the tread of a lonely master, but breathed a fragrance of flowers and a rippling murmur of well-contented song.

But the song was not from the throat of Bras-Coupé's wife. Silent and severe by day,

she moaned away whole nights, heaping re-
proaches upon herself for the impulse which
had permitted her hand to lie in Bras-Coupé's
and the priest to bind them together.

For in the audacity of her pride, or, as
Agricola would have said, in the immensity of
her impudence, she had held herself consecrate
to her hopeless love for Honoré Grandissime.
But now she was a black man's wife! and
even he unable to sit at her feet and learn the
lesson she had hoped to teach him. She had
heard of San Domingo, and for months the
fierce heart within her silent· bosom had been
leaping and shouting and seeing visions of fire
and blood, and when she brooded over the
nearness of Agricola and the remoteness of
Honoré, these visions got from her a sort of
mad consent. The lesson she would have
taught the giant was Insurrection. But it was
too late. Letting her dagger sleep in her bosom, and with an undefined belief in imaginary
resources, she had consented to join hands with
her giant hero before the priest; and when
the wedding had come and gone like a white
sail, she was seized with a lasting, fierce despair. A wild aggressiveness that had former-
ly characterized her glance in moments of an-
ger — moments which had grown more and

more infrequent under the softening influence
of her Mademoiselle's nature—now came back
intensified and blazed in her eye perpetually.
Whatever her secret love may have been in
kind, its sinking beyond hope below the horizon had left her fifty times the mutineer she
had been before—the mutineer who has nothing to lose.

"She loves her prince," said the negroes.

"Simple creatures!" said the overseer, who
prided himself on his discernment, "she loves
nothing ; she hates Agricola ; it's a case of hate
at first sight—the strongest kind."

Both were partly right; her feelings were
wonderfully knit to the African ; and she now
dedicated herself to Agricola's ruin.

Don José, it has been said, endeavored to be
happy ; but now his heart was filled with the
fear that he was bewitched. The negroes said
that Bras-Coupé had cursed the land. Morning
after morning, the master looked out with apprehension toward his fields, until one night
the worm came upon the indigo, and between
sunset and sunrise every green leaf had been
eaten up, and there was nothing left for either
insect or apprehension to feed upon. . . .

Moreover, fever and death, to a degree unknown before, fell upon his slaves. Those to

whom life was spared—but to whom strength did not return—wandered about the place like scarecrows, looking for shelter, and made the very air dismal with the reiteration, " We are bewitched, the voudou's spells are on us." The ripple of song was hushed and the flowers fell upon the floor.   .   .   .

The overseer shook his head.

" It is that accursed alligator, Bras-Coupé, down yonder in the swamp."

And by and by the master was again smitten with the same belief. He and his neighbors put in their crops afresh. The spring waned, summer passed, the fevers returned, the year wore round, but no harvest smiled. "Alas!" cried the planters, " we are all poor men!" The worst among the worst were the fields of Bras-Coupé's master—parched and shrivelled. " He does not understand planting," said his neighbors, " neither does his overseer. Maybe, too, it is true, as he says, that he is voudoued."

One day, at high noon, the master was taken sick with fever.

The third noon after—the sad wife sitting by the bedside—suddenly, right in the centre of the room, with the open door behind him, stood the magnificent, half-nude form of Bras-Coupé. He did not fall down as the mistress's eye met his, though all his flesh quivered.   The master was lying with his eyes closed.   The fever had done a fearful three days' work.

" Bras-Coupé wants his wife ! "

The master started wildly and stared upon his slave.

"Bras-Coupé wants his wife !" repeated the black.

"Seize him !" cried the sick man, trying to rise.

But, though several servants had ventured in with frightened faces, none dared molest the giant.   The master turned his entreating eyes upon his wife, but she seemed stunned, and only covered her face with her hands and sat as if paralyzed by a foreknowledge of what was coming.

Bras-Coupé lifted his great black palm and commenced :

" May this house and all in it who are not women be accursed."

The master fell back upon his pillow with a groan of helpless wrath.

The African pointed his finger through the open window.

" May its fields not know the plough nor nourish the cattle that overrun it."

The domestics, who had thus far stood their

ground, suddenly rushed from the room like
stampeded cattle, and at that moment appeared
Palmyre.

"Speak to him," faintly cried the panting invalid.

She went firmly up to her husband and lifted
her hand. With an easy motion, but quick as
lightning, as a lion sets foot on a dog, he
caught her by the arm.

"Bras-Coupé wants his wife," he said, and
just then Palmyre would have gone with him
to the equator.

"You shall not have her!" gasped the master.

The African seemed to rise in height, and
still holding his wife at arm's length, resumed
his curse:

"May weeds cover the ground until the air
is full of their odor and the wild beasts of the
forest come and lie down under their cover."

With a frantic effort the master lifted himself
upon his elbow and extended his clenched fist
in speechless defiance; but his brain reeled, his
sight went out, and when again he saw, Palmyre and her mistress were bending over him,
the overseer stood awkwardly by, and Bras-
Coupé was gone.

The plantation became an invalid camp.
The words of the voudou found fulfilment on

every side. The plough went not out; the
herds wandered through broken hedges from
field to field and came up with staring bones
and shrunken sides; a frenzied mob of weeds
and thorns wrestled and throttled each other
in a struggle for standing-room — rag-weed,
smart-weed, sneeze-weed, bind-weed, iron-weed
—until the burning skies of midsummer
checked their growth and crowned their un-
shorn tops with rank and dingy flowers.

" Why, in the name of St. Francis," asked
the priest of the overseer, "didn't the Señora
use her power over the black scoundrel when
he stood and cursed that day ? "

" Why, to tell you the truth, father," said the
overseer, in a discreet whisper, " I can only
suppose she thought Bras-Coupé had half a
right to do it."

"Ah, ah, I see; like her brother, Honoré—
looks at both sides of a question—a miserable
practice; but why couldn't Palmyre use *her*
eyes? They would have stopped him."

" Palmyre? Why Palmyre has become the
best *monture* (Plutonian medium) in the parish.
Agricola Fusilier himself is afraid of her. Sir,
I think sometimes Bras-Coupé is dead and his
spirit has gone into Palmyre. She would rather
add to his curse than take from it."

"Ah!" said the jovial divine, with a fat smile, "whipping would help her case; the whip is a great sanctifier. I fancy it would even make a Christian of Bras-Coupé."

But Bras-Coupé kept beyond the reach, alike of the lash and of the Latin Bible.

By and by came a man with a rumor, whom the overseer brought to the master's sick-room, to tell that an enterprising Frenchman was attempting to produce a new staple in Louisiana, one that worms would not annihilate. It was that year of history when the despairing planters saw ruin hovering so close over them, that they cried out to heaven for succor. . . . "And if we," cried the newsbearer, "get the juice of the sugar-cane to crystallize, we shall yet save our lands and homes. Oh, Señor, it will make you strong again to see these fields all cane and the long rows of negroes and negresses cutting it, while they sing that song by which they count the canes they cut," and the bearer of good tidings sang it for very joy.

" And Honoré Grandissime is going to introduce it on his lands," said Don José.

" That is true," said Agricola Fusilier, coming in. . . .

The señor smiled.

" I have some good tidings, too," he said;
" my beloved lady has borne me a son."

" Another scion of the house of Grand——I
mean Martinez ! " exclaimed Agricola. " And
now, Don José, let me say that *I* have an item
of rare intelligence ! "

The don lifted his feeble head and opened
his inquiring eyes with a sudden, savage light
in them.

" No," said Agricola, " he is not exactly taken
yet, but they are on his track."

" Who ? "

" The police. We may say Bras-Coupé is
virtually in our grasp."

It was on a Sabbath afternoon that a band of
Choctaws, having just played a game of rac-
quette behind the city, and a similar game being
about to end between the white champions of
two rival faubourgs, the beating of tom-toms,
rattling of mules' jaw-bones and sounding of
wooden horns drew the populace across the
fields to a spot whose present name of Congo
Square still preserves a reminder of its old
barbaric pastimes. On a grassy plain, under
the ramparts, the performers of these hideous
discords sat upon the ground, facing each other,
and in their midst the dancers danced. They

danced in couples, a few at a time, throwing their bodies into the most startling attitudes and the wildest contortions, while the whole company of black lookers-on, incited by the tones of the weird music and the violent postur- ing of the dancers, swayed and writhed in pas- sionate sympathy, beating their breasts, palms and thighs in time with the bones and drums, and at frequent intervals lifting, in that wild African unison, no more to be described than forgotten, the unutterable songs of the African dances. The volume of sound rose and fell with the augmentation or diminution of the dancers' extravagances. Now a fresh man, young and supple, bounding into the ring, re- vived the flagging rattlers, drummers and trumpeters; now a wearied dancer, finding his strength going, gathered all his force at the cry of "Dance to the death!" rallied to a grand finale and with one magnificent antic, fell foaming at the mouth.

The amusement had reached its height. Many participants had been lugged out by the neck to avoid their being danced on, and the enthusiasm had risen to a frenzy, when there bounded into the ring the blackest of black men, an athlete of superb figure, in breeches of "Indienne"—the stuff used for slave women's best dresses—jingling with bells, his feet in moccasins, his tight, crisp hair decked out with feathers, a necklace of alligator's teeth rattling on his breast and a living serpent twined about his neck.

It chanced that but one couple was dancing. Whether they had been sent there by advice of Agricola is not certain. Snatching a tambourine from a bystander as he entered, the stranger thrust the male dancer aside, faced the woman and began a series of saturnalian antics, compared with which all that had gone before was tame and sluggish; and, as he finally leaped, with tinkling heels, clean over his bewildered partner's head, the multitude howled with rapture.

Ill-starred Bras-Coupé. He was in that extra-hazardous and irresponsible condition of mind and body known in the undignified present as "drunk again."

By the strangest fortune, if not, as we have just hinted, by some design, the man whom he had once deposited in the willow bushes, and the woman Clemence, were the very two dancers, and no other, whom he had interrupted. The man first stupidly regarded, next admiringly gazed upon, and then distinctly recognized, his former driver. Five minutes later, the Spanish police were putting their heads together to devise a quick and permanent capture; and in the midst of the sixth minute, as the wonderful fellow was rising in a yet more astounding leap than his last, a lasso fell about his neck and brought him, crashing like a burnt tree, face upward upon the turf.

"The runaway slave," said the old French code, continued in force by the Spaniards, "the runaway slave who shall continue to be so for one month from the day of his being denounced to the officers of justice, shall have his ears cut off and shall be branded with the flower-de-luce on the shoulder; and on a second offence of the same nature, persisted in during one month of his being denounced, he shall be hamstrung, and be marked with the flower-de-luce on the other shoulder. On the third offence, he shall die." Bras-Coupé had run away only twice. "But," said Agricola, "these slaves must be taught their place. Besides, there is Article 27 of the same code: 'The slave who, having struck his master, shall have produced a bruise, shall suffer capital punishment'—a very necessary law!" He concluded with a scowl upon Palmyre, who shot back a glance which he never forgot.

The Spaniard showed himself very merciful

—for a Spaniard; he spared the captive's life.
He might have been more merciful still; but
Honoré Grandissime said some indignant
things in the African's favor, and as much to
teach the Grandissimes a lesson as to punish
the runaway, he would have repented his clem-
ency, as he repented the momentary truce
with Agricola, but for the tearful pleading of
the señora and the hot, dry eyes of her maid.
Because of these he overlooked the .offence
against his person and estate, and delivered
Bras-Coupé to the law to suffer only the penal-
ties of the crime he had committed against society by attempting to be a free man.

We repeat it for the credit of Palmyre, that
she pleaded for Bras-Coupé. But what it cost
her to make that intercession, knowing that his
death would leave her free, and that if he lived
she must be his wife, let us not attempt to say.

In the midst of the ancient town, in a part
which is now crumbling away, stood the Cala-
boza, with its damp vaults, grated cells, iron
cages and its whips; and there, soon enough,
they strapped Bras-Coupé, face downward, and
laid on the lash. And yet not a sound came
from the mutilated but unconquered African to
annoy the ear of the sleeping city.

He was brought at sunrise to the plantation.

The air was sweet with the smell of the fields. The long-horned oxen that drew him and the naked boy that drove the team stopped before his cabin.

"You cannot put that creature in there," said the thoughtful overseer. "He would suffocate under a roof—he has been too long out-of-doors for that. Put him on my cottage porch." There, at last, Palmyre burst into tears and sank down, while before her on a soft bed of dry grass, rested the helpless form of the captive giant, a cloth thrown over his galled back, his ears shorn from his head, and the tendons behind his knees severed. His eyes were dry, but there was in them that unspeakable despair that fills the eye of the charger when, fallen in the battle, he gazes with sidewise-bended neck upon the ruin wrought upon him. His eye turned sometimes slowly to his wife. He need not demand her now—she was always by him.

There was much talk over him—much idle talk; no power or circumstance has ever been found that will keep a Creole from talking. He merely lay still under it with a fixed frown; but once some incautious tongue dropped the name of Agricola. The black man's eyes came so quickly round to Palmyre that she thought he would speak; but no; his words were all in his eyes. She answered their gleam with a fierce affirmative glance, whereupon he slowly bent his head and spat upon the floor.

There was yet one more trial of his wild nature. The command came from his master's sick-bed that he must lift the curse.

Bras-Coupé merely smiled. God keep thy enemy from such a smile !

The overseer, with a policy less Spanish than his master's, endeavored to use persuasion. But the fallen prince would not so much as turn one glance from his parted hamstrings. Palmyre was then besought to intercede. She made one poor attempt, but her husband was nearer doing her an unkindness than ever he had been before; he made a slow sign for silence —with his fist; and every mouth was stopped.

At midnight following, there came, on the breeze that blew from the mansion, a sound of running here and there, of wailing and sobbing —another Bridegroom was coming, and the Spaniard, with much such a lamp in hand as most of us shall be found with, neither burning brightly nor wholly gone out, went forth to meet Him.

"Bras-Coupé," said Palmyre, next evening,

speaking low in his mangled ear, "the master is dead; he is just buried. As he was dying, Bras-Coupé, he asked that you would forgive him."

The maimed man looked steadfastly at his wife. He had not spoken since the lash struck him, and he spoke not now; but in those large, clear eyes, where his remaining strength seemed to have taken refuge as in a citadel, the old fierceness flared up for a moment, and then, like an expiring beacon, went out.

" Is your mistress well enough by this time to venture here?" whispered the overseer to Palmyre. "Let her come. Tell her not to fear, but to bring the babe—in her own arms, tell her—quickly!"

The lady came, her infant boy in her arms, knelt down beside the bed of sweet grass and set the child within the hollow of the African's arm. Bras-Coupé turned his gaze upon it; it smiled, its mother's smile, and put its hand upon the runaway's face, and the first tears of Bras-Coupé's life, the dying testimony of his humanity, gushed from his eyes and rolled down his cheek upon the infant's hand. He laid his own tenderly upon the babe's forehead, then removing it, waved it abroad, inaudibly moved his lips, dropped his arm, and closed his eyes. The curse was lifted.

" The poor devil!" said the overseer, wiping his eyes and looking fieldward. " Palmyre, you must get the priest."

The priest came, in the identical gown in which he had appeared the night of the two weddings. To the good father's many tender questions, Bras-Coupé turned a failing eye that gave no answers; until, at length:

" Do you know where you are going ?" asked the holy man.

" Yes," answered his eyes, brightening.

" Where ? "

He did not reply; he was lost in contemplation, and seemed looking far away.

So the question was repeated.

" Do you know where you are going ?"

And again the answer of the eyes. He knew.

" Where ? "

The overseer at the edge of the porch, the widow with her babe, and Palmyre and the priest, bending over the dying bed, turned an eager ear to catch the answer.

" To—" the voice failed a moment; the departing hero essayed again ; again it failed; he tried once more, lifted his hand, and with an ecstatic, upward smile, whispered, " To—Africa!"—and was gone.

5

JEAN-AH POQUELIN *

In the first years of the present century, the newly-established American Government was the most hateful thing in Louisiana. The Creoles were still kicking at such vile innovations as the trial by jury, American dances, anti-smuggling laws, and the printing of the Governor's proclamation in English. The Anglo-American flood, that was presently to burst in a deluge of immigration upon the delta, had thus far been felt only as slippery leakage which made the Creole tremble for his footing. At this time there stood, a short distance above what is now Canal Street, and considerably back from the line of villas which fringed the river-bank, an old colonial plantation house half in ruin.

It stood aloof from civilization, the tracts that had once been its indigo-fields given over to their first noxious wildness, and grown up

* Pronounced Zhon-ah Po-keh-lan, with lan, as in *lang*, spoken very shortly and without the final sound of *g*.

into one of the horridest marshes within a circuit of fifty miles.

The house was of heavy cypress, lifted up on pillars, grim, solid, and spiritless, its massive build a strong reminder of days still earlier, when every man had been his own peace officer and the insurrection of the blacks a daily source of anxiety. Its dark, weatherbeaten roof and sides, were hoisted up above the jungly plain in a distracted way, like a gigantic ammunition wagon stuck in the mud and abandoned by some retreating army. Around it was a dense growth of low water willows, with half a hundred sorts of rank or thorny bushes, strangers alike to the "language of flowers" and to the botanist's Greek. They were hung with countless strands of discolored and prickly smilax, and the impassable mud below bristled with the dwarf palmetto. Two lone forest-trees, dead cypresses, stood in the centre of the marsh, dotted with roosting vultures. The shallow strips of water were hid by myriads of aquatic plants, under whose coarse and spiritless flowers, could one have seen it, was a harbor of reptiles, great and small, to make one shudder to the end of his days.

The house was on a slightly-raised spot, the

levee of a draining canal. The waters of this canal did not run; they crawled, and were full of big, ravening fish and alligators, that held it against all comers.

Such was the home of old Jean Marie Poquelin, once a wealthy indigo planter, standing high in the esteem of his small, proud circle of exclusively male acquaintances in the old city ; now a hermit, alike shunned by and shunning all who had ever known him. " The last of his line," said the gossips. His father lies under the floor of the St. Louis Cathedral, with the wife of his youth on one side, and the wife of his old age on the other. Old Jean visits the spot daily. His half-brother—alas ! there was a mystery; no one knew what had become of the gentle, young half-brother, more than thirty years his junior, whom once he seemed so fondly to love, but who, seven years ago, had disappeared suddenly, once for all, and left no clew of his fate.

They had seemed to live so happily in each other's love. No father, mother, wife, no kindred upon earth. The elder, a bold, frank, impetuous, chivalric adventurer ; the younger, a gentle, studious, book-loving recluse ; they lived upon the ancestral estate like mated birds, one always on the wing, the other always in the nest.

There was no trait in Jean Marie Poquelin, said the old gossips, for which he was so well known among his few friends as his fondness for his "little brother." "Jacques said this," and "Jacques said that;" he "would leave this or that, or anything to Jacques," for "Jacques was a scholar," and "Jacques was good," or "wise," or "just," or "far-sighted," as the nature of the case required; and "he should ask Jacques as soon as he got home," since Jacques was never elsewhere to be seen.

It was between the roving character of the one brother, and the bookishness of the other, that the estate fell into decay. Jean Marie, generous gentleman, gambled the slaves away one by one, until none was left, man or woman, but one old African mute.

The indigo-fields and vats of Louisiana had been generally abandoned as unremunerative. Certain enterprising men had substituted the culture of sugar; but while the hermit was too unenterprising to take so active a course, the other saw larger, and, at that time, equally respectable profits, first in smuggling, and later in the African slave-trade. What harm could he see in it? The whole people said it was vitally necessary, and to minister to a vital public necessity—good enough, certainly, and so he laid up many a doubloon, that made him none the worse in the public regard.

One day, old Jean Marie was about to start upon a voyage that was to be longer, much longer, than any that he had yet made. Jacques had begged him hard for many days not to go, but he laughed him off, and finally said, kissing him:

"Good-by, little brother."

"No," said Jacques, "I shall go with you."

They left the old hulk of a house in the sole care of the African mute, and went away to the Guinea coast together.

Two years after, old Poquelin came home without his vessel. He must have arrived at his house by night. No one saw him come. No one saw "his little brother;" rumor whispered that he, too, had returned, but he had never been seen again.

A dark suspicion fell upon the old slavetrader. No matter that the few kept the many reminded of the tenderness that had ever marked his bearing to the missing man. The many shook their heads. "You know he has a quick and fearful temper;" and "why does he cover his loss with mystery?" "Grief would out with the truth."

"But," said the charitable few, "look in his

face; see that expression of true humanity."
The many did look in his face, and, as he
looked in theirs, he read the silent question,
"Where is thy brother Abel?" The few were
silenced, his former friends died off, and the
name of Jean Marie Poquelin became a sym-
bol of witchery, crime, and hideous nursery
fictions.

The man and his house were alike shunned.
The snipe and duck hunters forsook the marsh,
and the wood-cutters abandoned the canal.
Sometimes the hardier boys who ventured out
there snake-shooting, heard a slow thumping of
oar-locks on the canal. They would look at
each other for a moment half in terror, half in
glee, then rush from their sport in haste to
assail with their gibes the unoffending, withered
old man who, in rusty attire, sat in the stern of
a skiff, rowed homeward by his white-headed
African mute.

"O Jean-ah Poquelin! O Jean-ah! Jean-
ah Poquelin!"

It was not necessary to utter more than that.
No hint of wickedness, deformity, or any physical or moral demerit; merely the name and
tone of mockery: "Oh, Jean-ah Poquelin!"
and while they tumbled one over another in
their needless haste to fly, he would rise care-

fully from his seat, while the aged mute, with downcast face, went on rowing, and rolling up his brown fist and extending it toward the urchins, would pour forth such an unholy broadside of French oaths and curses as would all but craze them with delight.

Among both blacks and whites the house was the object of a thousand superstitions. Every midnight, they affirmed, the will-o'-the-wisp came out of the marsh and ran in and out of the rooms, flashing from window to window. The story of some lads, whose word in ordinary statements was worthless, was generally credited, that the night they camped in the woods, rather than pass the place after dark, they saw, about sunset, every window blood-red, and on each of the four chimneys an owl sitting, which turned his head three times round, and moaned and laughed with a human voice. There was a bottomless well, everybody professed to know, beneath the sill of the big front door under the rotten veranda; whoever set foot upon that threshold disappeared forever in the depths below.

What wonder the marsh grew as wild as Africa! Take all the suburb Sainte Marie, and half the ancient city, you would not find one graceless dare-devil reckless enough to pass within a hundred yards of the house after nightfall.

The foreign races, pouring into old New Orleans, began to find the few streets named for the Bourbon princes too narrow for them. The wheel of fortune, beginning to whirl, threw them off beyond the ancient corporation lines, and sowed civilization and even trade upon the lands of the old Creole planters. Fields became roads, roads streets. Everywhere the leveller was peering through his glass, rodsmen were whacking their way through willow-brakes and rose-hedges, and the sweating Irishmen tossed the blue clay up with their long-handled shovels.

"Ha! that is all very well," quoth the Jean-Baptistes, feeling the reproach of an enterprise that asked neither co-operation nor advice of them, "but wait till they come yonder to Jean Poquelin's marsh; ha! ha! ha!" The supposed predicament so delighted them, that they put on a mock terror and whirled about in an assumed stampede, then caught their clasped hands between their knees in excess of mirth, and laughed till the tears ran; for whether the street-makers mired in the marsh, or contrived to cut through old "Jean-ah's" property, either event would be joyful. Mean-

time, a line of tiny rods, with bits of white paper in their split tops, gradually extended its
way straight through the haunted ground, and
across the canal diagonally.

"We shall fill that ditch," said the men in
mud-boots, and brushed close along the
chained and padlocked gate of the haunted
mansion. Ah, Jean-ah Poquelin, those were
not Creole boys, to be stampeded with a little
hard swearing.

He went to the Governor. That official
scanned the odd figure with no slight interest.
Jean Poquelin was of short, broad frame, with
a bronzed, leonine face. His brow was ample
and deeply furrowed. His eye, large and
black, was bold and open like that of a war-
horse, and his jaws shut together with the firm-
ness of iron. He was dressed in a suit of blue
cottonade, and his shirt unbuttoned and
thrown back from the throat and bosom, sailor-
wise, showed a herculean breast, hard and
grizzled. There was no fierceness or defiance
in his look, no harsh ungentleness, no symptom
of his unlawful life or violent temper; but
rather a peaceful and peaceable fearlessness.
Across the whole face, not marked in one or
another feature, but as it were laid softly upon
the countenance like an almost imperceptible

veil, was the imprint of some great grief. A careless eye might easily overlook it, but, once seen, there it hung—faint, but unmistakable.

The Governor bowed.

"You speak French?" asked the figure.

"I would rather talk English, if you can do so," said the Governor.

"My name, Jean Poquelin."

"How can I serve you, Mr. Poquelin?"

"My house is yondeh in swamp."

The Governor bowed.

"Dat swamp billong to me."

"Yes, sir."

"To me; Jean Poquelin; I h-own him me-self."

"Well, sir?"

"He don't billong to you; I get him from my father."

"That is perfectly true, Mr. Poquelin, as far as I am aware."

"You want to make street pass yondeh?"

"I do not know, sir; it is quite probable; but the city will repay you for any loss you may suffer—you will get paid, you understand."

"Street can't pass dare."

"You will have to see the city authorities about that, Mr. Poquelin."

A bitter smile came upon the old man's face:

" Pardon, you is not the Governor?"

" Yes."

" Ah, yes. You har the Governor — yes. Veh-well. I come to you. I tell you, street can't pass at my 'ouse."

"But you will have to see"—

" I come to you. You har the Governor. I know not the new laws. I ham a Fr-r-rench-a-man! Fr-rench-a-man have something go contrarie—he come at his Governor. I come at you. If me not had been bought from my king like black man in the hold time, ze King of France would-a-show to take care his men to make street in right places. But, I know; we billong to that President. I want you do somesin for me, eh?"

" What is it?" asked the patient Governor.

" I want you tell that President, street— can't—pass—at—my—'ouse."

" Have a chair, Mr. Poquelin;" but the old man did not stir. The Governor took a quill and wrote a line to a city official, introducing Mr. Poquelin, and asking for him every possible courtesy. He handed it to him, instructing him where to present it.

" Mr. Poquelin," he said, with a winning

smile, "tell me, is it your house that our Creole citizens tell such odd stories about?"

The old man glared sternly upon the speaker, and with immovable features said:

"You don't see me trade some Guinea nigga?"

"Oh, no."

"You don't see me make some smugglin'?"

"No, sir; not at all."

"But, I am Jean Marie Poquelin. I mind my hown bizniss. Dat all right? Adieu."

He put his hat on and withdrew. By and by, he stood, letter in hand, before the person to whom it was addressed. This person employed an interpreter.

"He say'," said the interpreter to the officer, " he come, to make you the fair warning how you muz not make the street pass at his 'ouse."

The officer remarked that " such impudence was refreshing ; " but the experienced interpreter translated freely.

"He say': 'Why you don't want?'" said the interpreter.

The old slave-trader answered at some length.

"He say'," said the interpreter, again turning to the officer, "that marsh is a too unhealthy for peopl' to live."

"But we expect to drain his old marsh; it's not going to be a marsh."

"He say'"—the interpreter explained to the visitor in French.

The old man answered tersely.

"He say' the canal is private canal," said the interpreter to the Governor.

"Oh! *that* old ditch; that's to be filled up. Tell the old man we're going to fix him up nicely."

Translation being duly made, the man in power was amused to see a thunder-cloud gathering on the old man's face.

"Tell him," he added, "by the time we finish, there'll not be a ghost left in his shanty."

The interpreter began to translate, but——

"I know, I know," said the old man, with an impatient gesture, and burst forth, pouring curses upon the United States, the President, the Territory of Orleans, Congress, the Governor and all his subordinates, striding out of the apartment as he cursed, while the object of his maledictions roared with merriment and rammed the floor with his foot.

"Why, it will make his old place worth ten dollars to one," said the official to the interpreter.

"'Tis not for de worse of de property," said the interpreter.

"I should guess not," said the other, whittling his chair—"seems to me as if some of these old Creoles would rather live in a crawfish hole than to have a neighbor."

"You know what make old Jean Poquelin make like that? I will tell you. You know——"

The interpreter was rolling a cigarette, and paused to light his tinder; then, as the smoke poured in a thick double stream from his nostrils, he said, in a solemn whisper:

"He is a witch."

"Ho, ho, ho!" laughed the other.

"You don't believe it? What you want to bet?" cried the interpreter, jerking himself half up and thrusting out one arm, while he bared it of its coat-sleeve with the hand of the other. "What you want to bet?"

"How do you know?" asked the official.

"Dass what I goin' to tell you. You know, one evening, I was shooting some cranes. I killed three; but I had trouble to fine them, it was becoming so dark. When I have them I start' to come home; then I got to pass at Jean Poquelin's house."

"Ho, ho, ho!" laughed the other, throwing his leg over the arm of his chair.

"Wait," said the interpreter. "I come

along slow, not making some noises; still, still "——

" And scared," said the smiling one.

" But, wait. I get all past the house. ' Ah!' I say; ' all right!' Then I see two thing' before! Hah! I get as cold and humide, and shake like a leaf. You think it was nothing? There I see, so plain as can be (though it was making nearly dark), I see Jean—Marie—Poque-lin walkin' right in front, and right there beside of him was something like a man—but not a man—white like paint!—I dropp' on the grass from scared — they pass'; so sure as I live 'twas the ghost of Jacques Poquelin, his brother!"

" Pooh!" said the listener.

" I'll put my han' in the fire," said the interpreter.

" But did you never think," asked the other, " that that might be Jack Poquelin, as you call him, alive and well, and, for some cause, hid away by his brother?"

" But there are no cause!" said the other, and the entrance of third parties changed the subject.

Some months passed and the street was opened. A canal was first dug through the marsh; the small one, which passed so close to

Jean Poquelin's house, was filled; and the street, or rather a sunny road, just touched a corner of the old mansion's door-yard. The morass ran dry. Its serpents slipped away through the bulrushes; the cattle, roaming freely upon its hardened surface, trampled down the under-growth. The bellowing frogs were driven westward. Lilies and the flower-de-luce sprang up in the place of reeds; smilax and poison-oak gave way to the purple-plumed ironweed and pink spiderwort; the bindweeds ran everywhere, blooming as they ran, and on one of the dead cypresses a giant creeper hung its green burden of foliage and lifted its scarlet trumpets. Sparrows and red-birds flitted through the bushes, and dewberries grew ripe beneath. Over all these came a sweet, dry smell of health which the place had not known since the sand of the Mississippi's overflows first lifted it from the sea.

But its owner did not build. Over the willow-brakes, and down the vista of the open street, bright new houses, some singly, some by ranks, were prying in upon the old man's privacy. They even settled down toward his southern side. First a wood-cutter's hut or two, then a market-gardener's shanty, then a painted cottage, and all at once the suburb

6

had flanked and half surrounded him and his dried-up marsh.

Ah! then the common people began to hate him. "The old tyrant!" "You don't mean an old *tyrant?*" "Well, then, why doesn't he build when the public need demands it? What does he live in that unneighborly way for?" "The old pirate!" "The old kidnapper!" How easily even the most ultra Louisianians put on the imported virtues of the North, when they could be brought to bear against the hermit. "There he goes, with the boys after him! Ah! ha! ha! Jean-ah Po-quelin! Ah! Jean-ah! Aha! aha! Jean-ah Marie! Jean-ah Poquelin! The old villain!" How merrily the swarming Américains echo the spirit of persecution! "The old fraud," they say—" pretends to live in a haunted house, does he? We'll tar and feather him some day. Guess we can fix him."

He cannot be rowed home along the old canal now; he walks. His strength has broken sadly of late, and the street urchins are ever at his heels. It is like the days when they cried: "Go up, thou bald-head," and the old man now and then turns and delivers ineffectual curses.

To the Creoles—to the incoming lower

class of superstitious Germans, Irish, Sicilians, and others—he became an omen and embodiment of public and private ill-fortune. Upon him all their superstitions gathered and grew. If a house caught fire, it was laid to his witchcraft. Did a woman go off in a fit, he had bewitched her. Did a child stray off for an hour, the mother shivered with the apprehension that Jean Poquelin had offered him to strange gods. The house was the subject of every bad boy's invention who loved to contrive ghostly lies. "As long as that house stands we shall have bad luck. Do you not see our peas and beans dying, our cabbages and lettuce going to seed and our gardens turning to dust, while every day you can see it raining in the woods? The rain will never pass old Poquelin's house. He keeps a charm to conjure with. He has conjured the whole suburb Sainte Marie. And why, the old wretch? Simply because our playful and innocent children call after him as he passes."

A "Building and Improvement Company," which had not yet started, "but was going to," and which had not, indeed, any tangible capital yet, but "was going to have some," joined the "Jean-ah Poquelin" war. The haunted property would be such a capital site for a market-house! They sent a committee to the old mansion to ask its occupant to sell. The committee never got beyond the chained gate and a very barren interview with the African mute. The President of the Board was then empowered (for he had studied French in Pennsylvania and was considered qualified) to call and persuade M. Poquelin to subscribe to the company's stock; but——

"Fact is, gentlemen," he said at the next meeting, "it would take us at least twelve months to make Mr. Pokaleen understand the rather original features of our system, and he wouldn't subscribe when we'd done; besides, the only way to see him is to stop him on the street."

There was a great laugh from the Board; they couldn't help it. "Better meet a bear robbed of her whelps," said one.

"You're mistaken as to that," said the President. "I did meet him, and stopped him, and found him quite polite. But I could get no satisfaction from him; the fellow wouldn't talk in French, and when I spoke in English he hoisted his old shoulders up, and gave the same answer to everything I said."

"And what was that?" asked one or two, impatient of the pause.

" That it ' don't worse w'ile?'"

" Oh! it isn't worth while, eh? Well, we think it is."

One of the Board said: " Mr. President, this market-house project, as I take it, is not alto-gether a selfish one; the community is to be benefited by it. We may feel that we are working in the public interest (the Board smiled knowingly), if we employ all possible means to oust this old nuisance from among us. You may know that at the time the street was cut through, this old Poquelann did all he could to prevent it. It was owing to a certain connection which I had with that affair that I heard a ghost story (smiles, followed by a sud-den dignified check)—ghost story, which, of course, I am not going to relate ; but I *may* say that my profound conviction, arising from a prolonged study of that story, is, that this old villain, John Poquelann, has his brother locked up in that old house. Now, if this is so, and we can fix it on him, I merely *suggest* that we can make the matter highly useful. I don't know," he added, beginning to sit down, "but that it is an action we owe to the community— hem!"

" How do you propose to handle the sub-ject?" asked the President.

"I was thinking," said the speaker, "that, as a Board of Directors, it would be unadvisable for us to authorize any action involving trespass; but if you, for instance, Mr. President, should, as it were, for mere curiosity, *request* some one, as, for instance, our excellent Secretary, simply as a personal favor, to look into the matter—this is merely a suggestion."

The Secretary smiled sufficiently to be understood that, while he certainly did not consider such preposterous service a part of his duties as secretary, he might, notwithstanding, accede to the President's request; and the Board adjourned.

Little White, as the Secretary was called, was a mild, kind-hearted little man, who, nevertheless, had no fear of anything, unless it was the fear of being unkind.

"I tell you frankly," he privately said to the President, "I go into this purely for reasons of my own."

The next day, a little after nightfall, one might have seen this little man slipping along the rear fence of the Poquelin place, preparatory to vaulting over into the rank, grass-grown yard, and bearing himself altogether more after the manner of a collector of rare

TARRYAWHILE, MR. CABLE'S HOME, NORTHAMPTON, MASS.

chickens than according to the usage of secretaries.

The picture presented to his eye was not calculated to enliven his mind. The old mansion stood out against the western sky, black and silent. One long, lurid pencil-stroke along a sky of slate was all that was left of daylight. No sign of life was apparent; no light at any window, unless it might have been on the side of the house hidden from view. No owls were on the chimneys, no dogs were in the yard.

He entered the place, and ventured up behind a small cabin which stood apart from the house. Through one of its many crannies he easily detected the African mute crouched before a flickering pine-knot, his head on his knees, fast asleep.

The little Secretary concluded to enter the mansion, and, with that view, stood and scanned it. The broad rear steps of the veranda would not serve him; he might meet some one midway. He was measuring, with his eye, the proportions of one of the pillars which supported it, and estimating the practicability of climbing it, when he heard a footstep. Some one dragged a chair out toward the railing, then seemed to change his mind and began to pace the veranda, his footfalls resounding on the dry boards with singular loudness.   Little White drew a step backward, got the figure between himself and the sky, and at once recognized the short, broad-shouldered form of old Jean Poquelin.

Little White sat down upon a billet of wood, and, to escape the stings of a cloud of mosquitoes, shrouded his face and neck in his handkerchief, leaving his eyes uncovered.

He had sat there but a moment when he noticed a strange, sickening odor, faint, as if coming from a distance, but loathsome and horrid.

Whence could it come? Not from the cabin; not from the marsh, for it was as dry as powder.   It was not in the air; it seemed to come from the ground.

Rising up, he noticed, for the first time, a few steps before him, a narrow footpath leading toward the house.   He glanced down it—ha! right there was some one coming — ghostly white!

Quick as thought, and as noiselessly, he lay down at full length against the cabin.   It was bold strategy, and yet there was no denying it, little White felt that he was frightened.   "It is not a ghost," he said to himself.   "I *know* it cannot be a ghost;" but the perspiration burst out at every pore, and the air seemed to thicken with heat. " It is a living man," he said in his thoughts. " I hear his footstep, and I hear old Poquelin's footsteps, too, separately, over on the veranda. I am not discovered; the thing has passed; there is that odor again; what a smell of death! Is it coming back? Yes. It stops at the door of the cabin. Is it peering in at the sleeping mute? It moves away. It is in the path again. Now it is gone." He shuddered. " Now, if I dare venture, the mystery is solved." He rose cautiously, close against the cabin, and peered along the path.

The figure of a man, a presence if not a body — but whether clad in some white stuff or naked, the darkness would not allow him to de-termine—had turned, and now, with a seeming painful gait, moved slowly from him. " Great Heaven! can it be that the dead do walk?" He withdrew again the hands which had gone to his eyes. The dreadful object passed be-tween two pillars and under the house. He listened. There was a faint sound as of feet upon a staircase; then all was still except the measured tread of Jean Poquelin walking on the veranda, and the heavy breathing of the mute slumbering in the cabin.

The little Secretary was about to retreat;
but as he looked once more toward the haunted
house, a dim light appeared in the crack of a
closed window, and presently old Jean Poquelin came, dragging his chair, and sat down
close against the shining cranny. He spoke in
a low, tender tone in the French tongue, making some inquiry. An answer came from
within. Was it the voice of a human? So unnatural was it—so hollow, so discordant, so unearthly—that the stealthy listener shuddered
again from head to foot; and, when something
stirred in some bushes near by—though it may
have been nothing more than a rat—and came
scuttling through the grass, the little Secretary
actually turned and fled. As he left the en-
closure he moved with bolder leisure through
the bushes; yet now and then he spoke aloud:
"Oh, oh! I see, I understand!" and shut his
eyes in his hands.

How strange that henceforth little White
was the friend and champion of Jean Poquelin!
In season and out of season—wherever a word
was uttered against him—the Secretary, with a
quiet, aggressive force that instantly arrested
gossip, demanded upon what authority the
statement or conjecture was made; but as he
did not condescend to explain his own remark,

able attitude, it was not long before the dis-
relish and suspicion which had followed Jean
Poquelin so many years fell also upon him.

It was only the next evening but one after
his adventure, that he made himself a source of
sullen amazement to one hundred and fifty
boys, by ordering them to desist from their
hallooing. Old Jean Poquelin, standing and
shaking his cane, rolling out his long-drawn
curses, paused and stared, then gave the Secretary a courteous bow and started on. The
boys, save one, from pure astonishment, ceased;
but a little Irish lad, more daring than any had
yet been, threw a big hurtling clod, that struck
old Poquelin between the shoulders and burst
like a shell. The enraged old man wheeled
with uplifted staff to give chase to the scam-
pering vagabond ; and—he may have tripped,
or he may not, but he fell full length. Little
White hastened to help him up, but he waved
him off with a fierce oath and, staggering to his
feet, resumed his way homeward. His lips
were reddened with blood.

Little White was on his way to the meeting
of the Board. He would have given all he
dared spend to have staid away, for he felt
both too fierce and too tremulous to brook the
criticisms that were likely to be made.

"I can't help it, gentlemen; I can't help you to make a case against the old man, and I'm not going to."

"We did not expect this disappointment, Mr. White."

"I can't help that, sir. No, sir; you had better not appoint any more investigations. Somebody'll investigate himself into trouble. No, sir; it isn't a threat, it is only my advice, but I warn you that whoever takes the task in hand will rue it to his dying day—which may be hastened, too."

The President expressed himself "surprised."

"I don't care a rush," answered little White wildly and foolishly. "I don't care a rush if you are, sir. No, my nerves are not disordered; my head's as clear as a bell. No, I'm *not* excited."

A Director remarked that the Secretary looked as though' he had awaked from a nightmare.

"Well, sir, if you want to know the fact, I have; and if you choose to cultivate old Poquelin's society you can have one, too."

"White," called a member who thought himself funny, but White did not notice. "White," he called again.

"What?" demanded White, with a scowl.

" Did you see the ghost? "

" Yes, sir; I did," cried White, hitting the table, and handing the President a paper which brought the Board to other business.

The story got among the gossips that some-body (they were afraid to say little White) had been to the Poquelin mansion by night and beheld something appalling. The rumor was but a shadow of the truth, magnified and dis-torted as is the manner of shadows. He had seen skeletons walking, and had barely escaped the clutches of one by making the sign of the cross.

Some madcap boys, with an appetite for the horrible, plucked up courage to venture through the dried marsh by the cattle-path, and come before the house at a spectral hour when the air was full of bats. Something which they but half saw—half a sight was enough—sent them tearing back through the willow brakes and acacia bushes to their homes, where they fairly dropped down and cried:
· " Was it white? " " No—yes—nearly so—we can't tell—but we saw it." And one could hardly doubt, to look at their ashen faces, that they had, whatever it was.

" If that old rascal lived in the country we come from," said certain Américains, " he'd have been tarred and feathered before now, wouldn't he, Sanders?"

" Well, now, he just would."

"And we'd have rid him on a rail, wouldn't we?"

" That's what I allow."

" Tell you what you *could* do." They were talking to some rollicking Creoles who had assumed an absolute necessity for doing *something*. "What is it you call this thing where an old man marries a young girl, and you come out with horns and "——

" *Charivari?* " asked the Creoles.

"Yes, that's it. Why don't you shivaree him?" Happy thought!

Little White, with his wife beside him, was sitting on their doorsteps on the sidewalk, as Creole custom had taught them, looking toward the sunset. They had moved into the lately-opened street. The view was not attractive on the score of beauty. The houses were small and scattered, and across the flat commons, spite of the lofty tangle of weeds and bushes, and spite of the thickets of acacia, they needs must see the dismal old Poquelin mansion, tilted awry and shutting out the declining sun. The moon, white and slender, was hanging the tip of its horn over one of the chimneys,

" And you say," said the Secretary, " the old black mute has been going by here alone? Patty, suppose old Poquelin should be cooking up some mischief; he doesn't lack cause; the way that clod hit him the other day was enough to have killed him. Why, Patty, he dropped as quick as *that !* No wonder you haven't seen him. I wonder if they haven't heard something about him up at the drug-store. Suppose I go and see."

" Do," said his wife.

She sat alone for half an hour, watching that sudden going out of the day peculiar to the South.

" That moon is ghost enough for one house," she said, as her husband returned. " It has gone right down the chimney."

" Patty," said little White, " the drug-clerk says the boys are going to shivaree old Poquelin to-night. I'm going to try to stop it."

" Why, White," said his wife, " you'd better not. You'll get hurt."

" No, I'll not."

" Yes, you will."

" I'm going to sit out here until they come along. They're compelled to pass right by here."

" Why, White, it may be midnight before

they start; you're not going to sit out here till then."

" Yes, I am."

" Well, you're very foolish," said Mrs. White, in an undertone, looking anxious, and tapping one of the steps with her foot.

They sat a very long time talking over little family matters.

" What's that?" at last said Mrs. White.

" That's the nine-o'clock gun," said White, and they relapsed into a long, drowsy silence.

" Patty, you'd better go in and go to bed," said he, at last.

" I'm not sleepy."

" Well, you're very foolish," quietly remarked little White, and again silence fell upon them.

" Patty, suppose I walk out to the old house and see if I can find out anything."

" Suppose," said she, " you don't do any such —listen!"

Down the street arose a great hubbub. Dogs and boys were howling and barking; men were laughing, shouting, groaning, and blowing horns, whooping, and clanking cow-bells, whinnying, and howling, and rattling pots and pans.

" They are coming this way," said little

White. " You had better go into the house,
Patty."

" So had you."

" No. I'm going to see if I can't stop
them."

" Why, White ! "

" I'll be back in a minute," said White, and
went toward the noise.

In a few moments the little Secretary met
the mob. The pen hesitates on the word, for
there is a respectable difference, measurable
only on the scale of the half century, between
a mob and a *charivari.* Little White lifted his
ineffectual voice. He faced the head of the
disorderly column, and cast himself about as if
he were made of wood and moved by the jerk
of a string. He rushed to one who seemed,
from the size and clatter of his tin pan, to be a
leader. " *Stop these fellows, Bienvenu, stop them
just a minute, till I tell them something.*" Bienvenu turned and brandished his instruments of
discord in an imploring way to the crowd.
They slackened their pace, two or three hushed
their horns and joined the prayer of little
White and Bienvenu for silence. The throng
halted. The hush was delicious.

" Bienvenu," said little White, " don't shivaree old Poquelin to-night; he's"——

7

"My friend," said the swaying Bienvenu, "who tell you I goin' to charivari somebody, eh? You suppose because I make a little playful on this tin pan that I am drunk?"

"Oh, no, Bienvenu, old fellow, you're all right. I was afraid you might not know that old Poquelin was sick, you know; but you're not going there, are you?"

"My friend, I am very sorree to tell you that you are so drunk like a fool. I am ashame' of you. I am the servant of the public. These citizen' are going to ask Jean Poquelin to give to the Ursuline' at the hospital two hondred fifty dolla' "——

"Hey, what?" cried a listener. "*Five* hondred dolla', yes!"

"Yes," said Bienvenu, "and if he riffuse we make him some little music; ta-ra-ta!" He hoisted a merry hand and foot, then frowning, added: "Old Poquelin got no bizniz drink s'much whiskey."

"But, gentlemen," said little White, around whom a circle had gathered, "the old man is very sick."

"My faith!" cried a tiny Creole, "we did not make him to be sick. W'en we have say we going make the *charivari*, do you want that we all tell a lie? My faith!"

" But you can shivaree somebody else," said desperate little White.

" Yes! " cried Bienvenu, " and *charivari* Jean-ah Poquelin to-morrow ! "

" Let us go to Madame Schneider ! " cried two or three, and amid huzzas and confused cries, among which was heard a stentorian Celtic call for drinks, the crowd again began to move.

" One hondred dolla' for the Charity Hospital ! "

" Hurrah ! "

" One hondred dolla' for Charity Hospital ! "

" Hurrah ! "

" Whang ! " went a tin pan, the crowd yelled, and Pandemonium gaped again.   They were off at a right angle.

Nodding, Mrs. White looked at the mantle-clock.

" Well, if it isn't away after midnight."

The hideous noise down street was passing beyond earshot. She raised a sash and listened. For a moment there was silence. Some one came to the door.

" Is that you, White ? "

" Yes."   He entered.   " I succeeded, Patty."

" Did you ? " said Patty, joyfully.

" Yes.   They've gone down to shivaree the

old Dutchwoman who married her step-daughter's sweetheart. They say she has got to pay a hundred dollars to the hospital before they stop."

The couple retired, and Mrs. White slumbered. She was awakened by her husband snapping the lid of his watch.

"What time?" she asked.

"Half-past three. Patty, I haven't slept a wink. Those fellows are out yet. Don't you hear them?"

"Why, White, they're coming this way!"

"I know they are," said White, sliding out of bed and drawing on his clothes, "and they're coming fast. You'd better go away from that window, Patty. My! what a clatter!"

"Here they are," said Mrs. White, but her husband was gone. Two or three hundred men and boys pass the place at a rapid walk straight down the broad, new street, toward the hated house of ghosts. The din was terrific. She saw little White at the head of the rabble, brandishing his arms and trying in vain to make himself heard; but they only shook their heads, laughing and hooting the louder, and so passed, bearing him on before them.

Swiftly they pass out from among the houses, away from the dim oil lamps of the street, out into the broad starlit commons, and enter the willowy jungles of the haunted ground. Some hearts fail and their owners lag behind and turn back, suddenly remembering how near morning it is. But the most part push on, tearing the air with their clamor.

Down ahead of them, in the long, thicket-darkened way, there is—singularly enough—a faint, dancing light. It must be very near the old house; it is. It has stopped now. It is a lantern, and is under a well-known sapling which has grown up on the wayside since the canal was filled. Now it swings mysteriously to and fro. A goodly number of the more ghost-fearing give up the sport; but a full hundred move forward at a run, doubling their fiendish howling and banging.

Yes; it is a lantern, and there are two persons under the tree. The crowd draws near—drops into a walk; one of the two is the old African mute; he lifts the lantern up so that it shines on the other; the crowd recoils; there is a hush of all clangor, and all at once, with a cry of mingled fright and horror from every throat, the whole throng rushes back, dropping everything, sweeping past little White and hurrying on, never stopping until the jungle is left behind, and then to find that not one in ten has seen the cause of the stampede, and not one of the ten is certain what it was.

There is one huge fellow among them who looks capable of any villany. He finds something to mount on, and, in Creole-French, calls a general halt. Bienvenu sinks down, and, vainly trying to recline gracefully, resigns the leadership. The herd gather round the speaker; he assures them that they have been outraged. Their right peaceably to walk the public streets has been trampled upon. Shall such things be endured? It is now daybreak. Let them go now by the open light of day and force a free passage of the public highway!

A scattering consent was the response, and the crowd, thinned now and drowsy, straggled quietly down toward the old house. Some drifted ahead, others sauntered behind, but every one, as he again neared the tree, came to a standstill. Little White sat upon a bank of turf on the opposite side of the way, looking very stern and sad. To each new-comer he put the same question:

"Did you come here to go to old Poquelin's?"

" Yes."

" He's dead." And if the shocked hearer started away he would say: " Don't go away."

" Why not ? "

" I want you to go to the funeral presently."

If some Louisianian, too loyal to dear France or Spain to understand English, looked bewildered, some one would interpret for him ; and presently they went. Little White led the van, the crowd trooping after him down the middle of the way. The gate, that had never been seen before unchained, was open. Stern little White stopped a short distance from it ; the rabble stopped behind him. Something was moving out from under the veranda. The many whisperers stretched upward to see. The African mute came very slowly toward the gate, leading, by a cord in the nose, a small brown bull, which was harnessed to a rude cart. On the flat body of the cart, under a black cloth, were seen the outlines of a long box.

" Hats off, gentlemen," said little White, as the box came in view, and the crowd silently uncovered.

" Gentlemen," said little White, " here come the last remains of Jean Marie Poquelin, a bet-

ter man, I'm afraid, with all his sins—yes a
better—a kinder man to his blood—a man of
more self-forgetful goodness—than all of you
put together will ever dare to be."

There was a profound hush as the vehicle
came creaking through the gate; but when it
turned away from them toward the forest,
those in front started suddenly. There was a
backward rush, then all stood still again staring one way; for there, behind the bier, with
eyes cast down and labored step, walked the
living remains — all that was left — of little
Jacque Poquelin, the long-hidden brother —
a leper, as white as snow.

Dumb with horror, the cringing crowd gazed
upon the walking death. They watched, in
silent awe, the slow procession creep down the
long, straight road and lessen on the view, until, by and by, it stopped where a wild, unfre-
quented path branched off into the undergrowth
toward the rear of the ancient city.

"They are going to the Leper's Land," said
one in the crowd. The rest watched them in
silence.

The little bull was set free; the mute, with
the strength of an ape, lifted the long box to
his shoulder. For a moment more the mute
and the leper stood in sight, while the former

adjusted his heavy burden ; then, without one backward glance upon the unkind, human world, turning their faces toward the ridge in the depths of the swamp known as the Leper's Land, they stepped into the jungle, disappeared, and were never seen again.

NEW ORLEANS BEFORE THE CAPTURE.

IN the spring of 1862 we boys of New Orleans had no game. Nothing was "in;" none of the old playground sports that commonly fill the school-boy's calendar. We were even tired of drilling. Not one of us between seven and seventeen but could beat the drum, knew every bugle-call, and could go through the manual of arms and the facings like a drill-sergeant. We were *blasé* old soldiers—military critics.

Who could tell us anything? I recall but one trivial admission of ignorance on the part of any lad. On a certain day of grand review, when the city's entire defensive force was marching through Canal Street, there came along a stately body of tall, stalwart Germans, clad from head to foot in velveteen of a peculiarly loud smell, and a boy, spelling out their name upon their banner, said:

"H-u-s-s-a-r-s; what's them?"

"Aw, you fool!" cried a dozen urchins at once, "them's the Hoosiers; don't you smell 'em?"

But now the day of grand reviews was past. Hussars, Zouaves, and numberless other bodies of outlandish name had gone to the front in Tennessee and Virginia. Our cultivated eyes were satisfied now with one uniform that we saw daily. Every afternoon found us around in Coliseum Place, standing or lying on the grass, watching the dress parade of the "Confederate Guards." Most of us had fathers or uncles in the long, spotless, gray, white-gloved ranks that stretched down the hard, harsh turf of our old ball-ground.

This was the flower of the home guard. The merchants, bankers, underwriters, judges, real-estate owners, and capitalists, of the Anglo-American part of the city, were "all present or accounted for" in that long line. Gray heads, hoar heads, high heads, bald heads. Hands flashed to breast and waist with rigid precision at the command of "Present arms,"—hands that had ruled by the pen—the pen and the dollar—since long before any of us young spectators was born, and had done no harder muscular work than carve roasts and turkeys these twenty, thirty, forty years. Here and there among them were individuals who, unaided, had clothed and armed companies, squadrons, battalions, and sent them to the Cumberland and the Potomac. A good three-fourths of them had sons on distant battle-fields, some living, some dead.

We boys saw nothing pathetic in this array of old men. To us there was only rich enjoyment in the scene. If there was anything solemn about it, why did the band play polkas? Why was the strain every day the same gay

Tra la la, tra la la, tra la la la la......................

Away down to the far end of the line and back again, the short, stout German drum major, holding his gaudy office in this case by virtue of his girth, not height, flourished his big stick majestically, bursting with rage at us for carelessly repeating at short intervals in his hearing that "He kot it mit his size."

In those beautiful spring afternoons there was scarcely a man to be found, anywhere, out of uniform. Down on the steamboat landing, our famous Levee, a superb body of Creoles drilled and paraded in dark-blue. The orders were given in French; the movements were quick, short, nervy. The "about march"

was four sharp stamps of their neatly shod feet
—*one, two, three, four*—that brought them face
about and sent them back, tramp, tramp, tramp,
over the smooth, white pavement of powdered
oyster-shells. Ah! the nakedness of that once
crowded and roaring market-place.

And there was a "Foreign Legion." Of
course, the city had always been full of for-
eigners; but now it was a subject of amazement, not unmixed with satire, to see how
many, whom everyone had supposed to be
Americans or "citizens of Louisiana," bloomed
out as British, or French, or Spanish subjects.
But even so, the tremendous pressure of popular sentiment crowded them into the ranks and
forced them to make every show of readiness
to "hurl back the foe," as we used to call it.
And they really served for much. Merely as
a police force they relieved just as many Confederate soldiers of police duty in a city under
martial law, and enabled them to man forts and
breastworks at short notice, whenever that call
should come.

That call, the gray heads knew, was coming.
They confessed the conviction softly to one
another in the counting-rooms and idle store-
fronts when they thought no one was listening.
I used to hear them—standing with my back

turned, pretending to be looking at something down street, but with both ears turned backward and stretched wide. They said under their breath that there was not a single measure of defense that was not behindhand. And they spoke truly. In family councils a new domestic art began to be studied and discussed —the art of hiding valuables.

There had come a great silence upon trade. Long ago the custom warehouses had first begun to show a growing roominess, then emptiness, and then had remained shut, and the iron bolts and cross-bars of their doors were gray with cobwebs. One of them, where I had earned my first wages as a self-supporting lad, had been turned into a sword-bayonet factory, and I had been turned out. For some time later the Levee had kept busy; but its stir and noise had gradually declined, faltered, turned into the commerce of war and the clatter of calkers and ship-carpenters, and faded out. Both receipts and orders from the interior country had shrunk and shrunk, and the brave, steady fellows, who, at entry and shipping and cash and account desks, could no longer keep up a show of occupation, had laid down the pen, taken up the sword and musket, and followed after the earlier and

more eager volunteers. There had been one
new, tremendous sport for moneyed men for
a while, with spoils to make it interesting.
The seagoing tow-boats of New Orleans were
long, slender side-wheelers, all naked power
and speed, without either freight or passenger
room, each with a single, tall, slim chimney
and hurrying walking-beam, their low, taper
hulls trailing behind, scarcely above the water,
and perpetually drenched with the yeast of
the wheels. Some merchants of the more
audacious sort, restless under the strange new
quiet of their streets, had got letters of mark
and reprisal (the right, that is, to capture an
enemy's ships), and let slip these sharp-nosed
deerhounds upon the tardy, unsuspecting ships
that came sailing up to the Passes, unaware of
any declaration of war. But that game, too,
was up. The blockade had closed in like a
prison gate; the lighter tow-boats, draped
with tarpaulins, were huddled together under
Slaughterhouse Point, with their cold boilers
and motionless machinery yielding to rust;
the more powerful ones had been moored at
the long wharf vacated by Morgan's Texas
steamships; there had been a great hammer-
ing, and making of chips, and clatter of railroad iron, turning these tow-boats into iron-

clad cotton gun-boats, and these had crawled away, some up and some down the river, to be seen in that harbor no more. At length, only the foundries, the dry-docks across the river, and the ship-yard in suburb Jefferson, where the great ram *Mississippi* was being too slowly built, were active, and the queen of Southern commerce, the city that had once believed it was to be the greatest in the world, was absolutely out of employment.

There was, true, some movement of the sugar and rice crops into the hands of merchants who had advanced the money to grow them; and the cotton-presses and cotton-yards were full of cotton, but there it all stuck; and when one counts in a feeble exchange of city for country supplies, there was nothing more. Except—yes—that the merchants had turned upon each other, and were now engaged in a mere passing back and forth among themselves in speculation the daily diminishing supply of goods and food. Some were too noble to take part in this, and dealt only with consumers. I remember one odd little old man, an extensive wholesale grocer, who used to get tipsy all by himself every day, and go home so, but who would not speculate on the food of a distressed city. He had not got down to that.

Gold and silver had long ago disappeared. Confederate money was the currency; and not merely was the price of food and raiment rising, the value of the money was going down. The State, too, had a paper issue, and the city had another. Yet with all these there was first a famine of small change, and then a deluge of private paper money, called "shinplasters." Pah! What a mess it was! The boss butchers and the keepers of drinking-houses actually took the lead in issuing "money." The current joke was that you could pass the label of an olive oil bottle, because it was greasy, smelt bad, and bore an autograph. I did my first work as a cashier in those days, and I can remember the smell of my cash drawer yet. Instead of five-cent pieces we had car-tickets. How the grimy little things used to stick together! They would pass and pass until they were so soft and illegible with grocers' and butchers' handling that you could tell only by some faint show of their original color what company had issued them. Rogues did a lively business in "split tickets," literally splitting them and making one ticket serve for two.

Decay had come in. In that warm, moist climate it is always hungry, and, wherever it is allowed to feed, eats with a greed that is strange to see. With the wharves, always expensive and difficult to maintain, it made havoc. The occasional idle, weather-stained ship moored beside them, and resting on the water almost as light and void as an empty peascod, could hardly find a place to fasten to. The streets fell into sad neglect, but the litter of commerce was not in them, and some of their round-stone pavements, after a shower, would have the melancholy cleanness of weather-bleached bones. How quiet and lonely the harbor grew! The big dry-docks against the farther shore were all empty. Now and then a tug fussed about, with the yellow river all to itself; and one or two steamboats came and went each day, but they moved drowsily, and, across on the other side of the river, a whole fleet of their dingy white sisters lay tied up to the bank *sine die*. My favorite of all the sea-steamers, the little *Habana*, that had been wont to arrive twice a month from Cuba, disgorge her Spanish-American cargo, and bustle away again, and that I had watched the shipwrights, at their very elbows, razee and fit with three big, raking masts in place of her two small ones, had long ago slipped down the river and through the blockaders, and was now no longer the *Habana*, but the far-famed and dreaded *Sumter*.

The movements of military and naval defense lent some stir. The old revenue-cutter *Washington*, a graceful craft, all wings, no steam, came and went from the foot of Canal Street. She was lying there the morning Farragut's topmasts hove in sight across the low land at English Turn. Near by, on her starboard side, lay a gun-boat, moored near the spot where the "lower coast" packet landed daily; to which spot the crowd used to rush sometimes to see the commanding officer, Major-General Mansfield Lovell, ride aboard, bound down the river to the forts. Lovell was a lithe, brown-haired man of forty-odd, a very attractive figure, giving the eye, at first glance, a promise of much activity. He was a showy horseman, visibly fond of his horse. He rode with so long a stirrup-leather that he simply stood astride the saddle, as straight as a spear; and the idlers of the landing loved to see him keep the saddle and pass from the wharf to the steamboat's deck on her long, narrow stage-plank, without dismounting.

Such petty breaks in the dreariness got to be scarce and precious toward the last. Not that the town seemed so desolate then as it does now, as one tells of it; but the times were grim. Opposite the rear of the store where I was now employed—for it fronted in Common Street and stretched through to Canal—the huge, unfinished custom-house reared its lofty granite walls, and I used to go to its top, now and then, to cast my eye over the broad city and harbor below. When I did so, I looked down upon a town that had never been really glad again after the awful day of Shiloh. She had sent so many gallant fellows to help Beauregard, and some of them so young—her last gleaning—that when, on the day of their departure, they marched with solid column and firm-set, unsmiling mouths down the long gray lane made by the open ranks of those old Confederate guards, their escort broke into cheers and tears. They waved their gray shakoes on the tops of their bayonets and seized the dear lads' hands as they passed in mute self-devotion and steady tread, while the trumpets sang " Listen to the Mocking-bird." That was the last time; the town never cheered with elation afterward; and when the people next uncovered it was in silence, to let the body of Albert Sidney Johnston, their great chevalier, pass slowly up St. Charles Street behind the muffled drums, while on their quivering hearts was written with a knife the death-roll of that lost battle. One of those who had brought that precious body—a former schoolmate of mine—walked beside the bier, with the stains of camp and battle on him from head to foot. The war was coming very near.

Many of the town's old forms and habits of peace held fast. The city, I have said, was under martial law ; yet the city management still went through its old routines. The volunteer fire department was as voluntary and as riotous as ever. The police courts, too, were as cheerful as of old. The public schools had merely substituted "Dixie," the "Marseillaise," and the " Bonnie Blue Flag" for " Hail, Columbia" and the " Star-Spangled Banner," and were running straight along. There was one thing besides, of which many of us knew nothing at the time—a spy system, secret, diligent and fierce, that marked down every man suspected of sympathy with the enemy in a book whose name was too vile to find place on any page. This was not the military secret service —that is to be expected wherever there is war —nor any authorized police, but the scheme of some of the worst of the villains who had ruled New Orleans with the rod of terror for many years—the " Thugs."

But the public mind was at a transparent heat. Everybody wanted to know of every-

body else, " Why don't you go to the front?"
Even the gentle maidens demanded tartly, one
of another, why each other's brothers or lovers
had not gone long ago.   Whereas, in truth, the
laggards were few indeed.   The very children
were fierce.   For now even we, the uninformed,
the lads and women, knew the enemy was closing down upon us.   Of course, we confronted
the fact very valorously, we boys and mothers
and sisters—and the newspapers.   Had we not
inspected the fortifications ourselves?   Was
not every man in town ready to rush into
them at the twelve taps of the fire-alarm
bells?   Were we not ready to man them if
the men gave out?   Nothing afloat could pass
the forts.   Nothing that walked could get
through our swamps.   The *Mississippi*—and,
in fact, she was a majestically terrible struct-
ure, only let us *complete* her—would sweep the
river clean !

But there was little laughter.   Food was
dear; the destitute poor were multiplying ter-
ribly; the market men and women, mainly
Germans, Gascon-French and Sicilians, had
lately refused to take the shinplaster currency,
and the city authority had forced them to accept it.   There was little to laugh at.   The
Mississippi was gnawing its levees and threat-

ening to plunge in upon us. The city was believed to be full of spies.

I shall not try to describe the day the alarm-
bells told us the city was in danger and called
every man to his mustering-point. The children poured out from the school gates and ran
crying to their homes, meeting their sobbing
mothers at their thresholds. The men fell into
ranks. I was left entirely alone in charge of
the store where I was employed. Late in the
afternoon, receiving orders to close it, I did so,
and went home. But I did not stay. I went to
the river-side. There, until far into the night,
I saw hundreds of drays carrying cotton out of
the presses and yards to the wharves, where it
was fired. The glare of those serpentine miles
of flame set men and women weeping and wailing thirty miles away on the farther shore of
Lake Pontchartrain. But the next day was the
day of terrors. During the night fear, wrath
and sense of betrayal had run through the
people as the fire had run through the cotton.
You have seen, perhaps, a family fleeing with
lamentations and wringing of hands out of a
burning house; multiply it by thousands upon
thousands: that was New Orleans, though the
houses were not burning. The firemen were
out; but they cast fire on the waters, putting

the torch to the empty ships and cutting them loose to float down the river.

Whoever could go was going. The great mass, that had no place to go to or means to go with, was beside itself. "Betrayed! betrayed!" it cried, and ran in throngs from street to street, seeking some vent, some victim for its wrath. I saw a crowd catch a poor fellow at the corner of Magazine and Common Streets, whose crime was that he looked like a stranger and might be a spy. He was the palest living man I ever saw. They swung him to a neighboring lamp-post, but the Foreign Legion was patrolling the town in strong squads, and one of its lieutenants, all green and gold, leaped with drawn sword, cut the rope, and saved the man. This was one occurrence; there were many like it. I stood in the rear door of our store, Canal Street, soon after reopening it. The junior of the firm was within. I called him to look toward the river. The masts of the cutter *Washington* were slowly tipping, declining, sinking—down she went. The gunboat moored next her began to smoke all over and then to blaze. My employers lifted up their heels and left the city—left their goods and their affairs in the hands of one mere lad— no stranger would have thought I had reached

fourteen — and one big German porter. I
closed the doors, sent the porter to his place in
the Foreign Legion, and ran to the levee to see
the sights.

What a gathering! The riff-raff of the
wharves, the town, the gutters. Such women
—such wrecks of women! And all the juve-
nile rag-tag. The lower steamboat landing,
well covered with sugar, rice and molasses,
was being rifled. The men smashed; the
women scooped up the smashings. The river
was overflowing the top of the levee. A rain-
storm began to threaten. "Are the Yankee
ships in sight?" I asked of an idler. He
pointed out the tops of their naked masts as
they showed up across the huge bend of the
river. They were engaging the batteries at
Camp Chalmette—the old field of Jackson's
renown. Presently that was over. Ah, me!
I see them now as they come slowly round
Slaughterhouse Point into full view, silent,
grim and terrible, black with men, heavy with
deadly portent, the long-banished Stars and
Stripes flying against the frowning sky. Oh,
for the *Mississippi!* the *Mississippi!* Just then
here she came down upon them. But how?
Drifting helplessly, a mass of flames.

The crowds on the levee howled and

screamed with rage. The swarming decks answered never a word; but one old tar on the *Hartford*, standing with lanyard in hand beside a great pivot-gun, so plain to view that you could see him smile, silently patted its big black breech and blandly grinned.

And now the rain came down in sheets. About one or two o'clock in the afternoon came a roar of shoutings and imprecations and crowding feet down Common Street. "Hurrah for Jeff Davis! Hurrah for Jeff Davis! Shoot them! Kill them! Hang them!" I locked the door on the outside and ran to the front of the mob, bawling with the rest, "Hurrah for Jeff Davis!" About every third man there had a weapon out. Two officers of the United States Navy were walking abreast, unguarded and alone, looking not to right or left, never frowning, never flinching, while the mob screamed in their ears, shook cocked pistols in their faces, cursed and crowded and gnashed upon them. So, through the gates of death, those two men walked to the City Hall to demand the town's surrender. It was one of the bravest deeds I ever saw done.

Later events, except one, I leave to other pens. An officer from the fleet stood on the City Hall roof about to lower the flag of Lou-

isiana. In the street beneath gleamed the
bayonets of a body of marines. A howitzer
pointed up, and another down, the street. All
around swarmed the mob. Just then Mayor
Monroe—lest the officer above should be fired
upon and the howitzers open upon the crowd
—came out alone and stood just before one
of the howitzers, tall, slender, with folded arms,
eyeing the gunner. Down sank the flag.
Captain Bell, tall and stiff, marched off with
the flag rolled under his arm and the howitzers clanking behind. Then cheer after cheer
rang out for Monroe. And now, I daresay,
everyone is well pleased that, after all, New
Orleans never lowered her colors with her
own hands.

GREGORY'S ISLAND

THE man of whom I am speaking was a tall-ish, slim, young fellow, shaped well enough, though a trifle limp for a Louisianian in the Mississippi cavalry. Some camp wag had fastened on him the nickname of "Cracked-fiddle."

I met him first at the house of a planter, where I was making the most of a flesh-wound, and was in uniform myself simply because I hadn't any other clothes. There were pretty girls in the house, and as his friends and fellow-visitors—except me—wore the gilt bars of commissioned rank on their gray collars, and he, as a private, had done nothing glorious, his appearance was always in "citizen's" dress. Black he wore, from head to foot, in the cut fashionable in New Orleans when the war brought fashion to a stand : coat-waist short, skirt solemnly long ; sleeves and trousers small at the hands and feet, and puffed out—phew! in the middle. The whole scheme was dandy-ish, dashing, zouzou ; and when he appeared in it, dark, good-looking, loose, languorous, slow to smile and slower to speak, it was—confusing.

One sunset hour, as I sat alone on the planter's veranda immersed in a romance, I noticed, too late to offer any warning, this impressive black suit and its ungenerously nick-named contents coming in at the gate unprotected. Dogs, in the South, in those times, were not the caressed and harmless creatures now so common. A Mississippi planter's watch-dogs were kept for their vigilant and ferocious hostility to the negro of the quarters and to all strangers. One of these, a powerful, notorious, bloodthirsty brute, long-bodied, deer-legged, darted out of hiding and silently sprang at the visitor's throat. Gregory swerved, and the brute's fangs, whirling by his face, closed in the sleeve and rent it from shoulder to elbow. At the same time another, one of the old "bear-dog" breed, was coming as fast as the light block and chain he had to drag would allow him. Gregory neither spoke nor moved to attack or retreat. At my outcry the dogs slunk away, and he asked me, diffidently, for a thing which was very precious in those days—pins.

But he was quickly surrounded by pitying eyes and emotional voices, and was coaxed into the house, where the young ladies took his coat away to mend it. While he waited for it in my room I spoke of the terror so many brave men had of these fierce home-guards. I knew one such beast that was sired of a wolf. He heard me with downcast eyes, at first with evident pleasure, but very soon quite gravely.

" They can afford to fear dogs," he replied, " when they've got no other fear." And when I would have it that he had shown a stout heart, he smiled sadly.

" I do everything through weakness," he said to himself, and, taking my book, opened it as if to dismiss our theme. But I bade him turn to the preface, where we read something like this:

The seed of heroism is in all of us; else we should not forever relish, as we do, stories of peril, temptation, and exploit. Their true zest is no mere ticklement of our curiosity or wonder, but comradeship with souls that have courage in danger, faithfulness under trial, or magnanimity in triumph or defeat. We have, moreover, a care for human excellence *in general*, by reason of which we want not alone our son, or cousin, or sister, but *man everywhere*, the norm, *man*, to be strong, sweet, and true; and reading stories of such, we feel this wish rebound upon us as duty sweetened by a new hope, and have a new yearning for its fulfillment in ourselves.

"In short," said I, closing the book, "those imaginative victories of soul over circumstance become essentially ours by sympathy and emulation, don't they?"

"O yes," he sighed, and added an indistinct word about "spasms of virtue." But I claimed a special charm and use for unexpected and detached heroism, be they fact or fiction. "If virtue," I argued, "can spring up all of itself, from unsuspected seed and without the big roots of character—"

"You think," interrupted Gregory, "there's a fresh chance for me."

"For all the common run of us!" I cried. "Why not? And even if there isn't, hasn't it a beauty and a value? Isn't a rose a rose, on the bush or off? Gold is gold wherever you find it, and the veriest spasm of true virtue, coined into action, is true virtue and counts. It may not work my nature's whole redemption, but it works that way, and is just so much solid help toward the whole world's uplift." I was young enough then to talk in that manner, and he actually took comfort in my words, confessing that it had been his way to count a good act which was not in character with its doer, as something like a dead loss to everybody.

" I'm glad it's not," he said, " for I reckon my ruling motive is always fear."

" Was it fear this evening?" I asked.

" Yes," he replied, " it was. It was fear of a coward's name, and a sort of abject horror of being one."

" Too big a coward inside," I laughed, " to be a big, stout coward outside," and he assented.

" Smith," he said, and paused long, " if I were a hard drinker and should try to quit, it wouldn't be courage that would carry me through, but fear; quaking fear of a drunkard's life and a drunkard's death."

I was about to rejoin that the danger was already at his door, but he read the warning accusation in my eye.

" I'm afraid so," he responded. " I had a strange experience once," he presently added, as if reminded of it by what we had last said. " I took a prisoner."

" By the overwhelming power of fear?" I inquired.

" Partly, yes. I saw him before he saw me and I felt that if I didn't take him he'd either take me or shoot me, so I covered him and he surrendered. We were in an old pine clearing grown up with oak bushes."

" Would it have been less strange," I inquired, " if you had been in an old oak clearing grown up with pine bushes ? "

" No, he'd have got away just the same."

" What! you didn't bring him in ? "

" Only part of the way. Then he broke and ran."

" And you had to shoot him ? "

" No. I didn't even shoot at him. I couldn't, Smith; *he looked so much like me.* It was like seeing my own ghost. All the time I had him something kept saying to me, ' You're your own prisoner — you're your own prisoner.' And do you know—that thing comes back to me now every time I get into the least sort of a tight place ? "

" I wish it would come to me," I responded. A slave girl brought his coat and our talk remained unfinished until five years after the war.

Gregory had been brought up on the shore of the Mississippi Sound, a beautiful region fruitful mainly in weakness of character. He. was a skilled lover of sail-boats. When we all got back to New Orleans and cast about for a living in the various channels " open to gentlemen," he, largely, I think, owing to his timid notion of his worth, went into the rough business of owning and sailing a small, handsome schooner in the "Lake trade," which, you know, includes Mississippi Sound. I married, and for some time he liked much to come and see us—on rainy evenings, when he knew we should be alone. He was in love yet, as he had been when we were soldiers, and with the same girl. But his heart had never dared to hope, and the girl was of too true a sort ever to thrust hope upon him. What his love lacked in courage it made up in constancy, however, and morning, noon, and night —sometimes midnight, too, I venture to say— his all too patient heart had bowed mutely down toward its holy city across the burning sands of his diffidence. When another fellow stepped in and married her, he simply loved on, in the same innocent, dumb, harmless way as before.

He gave himself some droll consolations. One of these was a pretty, sloop-rigged sail-boat, trim and swift, on which he lavished the tendernesses he knew he should never bestow upon any living woman. He named her *Sweetheart;* a general term; but he knew that we all knew it meant the mender of his coat. By and by his visits fell off and I rarely met him except on the street. Sometimes we stopped for a moment's sidewalk chat, New Orleans fashion, and I still envied the clear bronze of his fine skin, which the rest of us had soon lost. But after a while certain changes began to show for the worse, until one day, in the summer of the fifth year, he tried to hurry by me. I stopped him, and was thinking what a handsome fellow he was even yet, with such a quiet, modest fineness about him, when he began, with a sudden agony of face, "My schooner's sold for debt! You know the reason; I've seen you read it all over me every time we have met, these twelve months—O *don't* look at me!"

His slim, refined hands—he gave me both—were clammy and tremulous. "Yes," he babbled on, "it's a fixed fact, Smith; the cracked fiddle's a smashed fiddle at last!"

I drew him out of the hot sun and into a secluded archway, he talking straight on with a speed and pitiful grandiloquence, totally unlike him. "I've finished all the easy parts—the first ecstasies of pure license—the long down-hill plunge, with all its mad exhilarations—the wild vanity of venturing—that bigness of the soul's experiences which makes

even its anguish seem finer than the old bit-
terness of tame propriety—I've gone through
all those things ; they are all behind me, now
—the valley of horrors is before ! You can't
understand it, Smith. O you can't understand it !"

O couldn't I! And, anyhow, one does not
have to put himself through a whole criminal
performance to know how it feels. I understood all, and especially what he showed even
now ; that deep thirst for the dramatic element
in one's own life, which, when social conformity
fails to supply it, becomes, to an eager soul,
sin's cunningest snare.

I tried to talk to him. "Gregory, that day
the dogs jumped on you—you remember ?—
didn't you say if ever you should reach this
condition your fear might save you ?"

He stared at me a moment. "Do you "—a
ray of humor lighted his eyes—"do you still
believe in spasms of virtue ?"

"Thank heaven, yes !" laughed I, and he
said good-by and was gone.

I heard of him twice afterward that day.
About noon, some one coming into the office
said : "I just now saw Crackedfiddle buying
a great lot of powder, and shot, and fishing-
tackle. Here's a note. He says first read it

and then seal it and send it to his aunt." It read :

"*Don't look for me. You can't find me. I'm not going to kill or hurt myself, and I'll report again in a month.*"

I delivered it in person on my way uptown, advising his kinswoman to trust him on his own terms and hope for the best. Privately, of course, I was distressed, and did not become less so when, on reaching home, my wife told me that he had been there and borrowed an arm-load of books, saying he might return some of them in a month, but would probably keep others for two. So he did ; and one evening, when he brought the last of them back, he told us fully what had happened to him in the interval.

The sale of the schooner had paid its debt and left him some cash over. Better yet, it had saved *Sweetheart*. On the day of his disappearance, she was lying at the head of the New Basin, distant but a few minutes' walk from the spot where we had met and talked. When he left me he went there. At the stores near by he bought a new hatchet and axe, an extra water-keg or two, and a month's provisions. He filled all the kegs, stowed everything aboard, and by the time the afternoon had half waned, was rippling down the New Canal under mule-tow with a strong lake breeze in his face.

At the lake (Pontchartrain), as the tow-line was cast off, he hoisted sail, and, skimming out by lighthouse and breakwater, tripped away toward the eastern skyline, he and *Sweet-heart* alone, his hand clasping hers—the tiller, that is—hour by hour, and the small waves tiptoeing to kiss her southern cheek as she leaned the other away from the saucy north wind. In time the low land and then the lighthouse sank and vanished behind them; on the left the sun went down in the purple-black swamps; the waters between turned crimson and bronze under the fairer changes of the sky, while in front of them, Fort Pike Light began to glimmer through an opal haze and, by and by, to draw near. It passed. From a large inbound schooner, gliding by in the twilight, came, in friendly recognition, the drone of a conch-shell, the last happy salutation *Sweet-heart* was ever to receive. Then the evening star silvered their wake through the deep Rig-olets, and the rising moon met them, her and her lover, in Lake Borgne, passing the dark pines of Round Island, and hurrying on toward the white sand-keys of the Gulf.

The night was well advanced as they neared
the pine-crested dunes of Cat Island, in whose
lee a more cautious sailor would have dropped
anchor till the morning. But to this pair every
mile of these fickle waters, channel and mud-
lump, snug lagoon, open sea and hidden bar,
each and all, were known as the woods are
known to a hunter, and, as he drew her hand
closer to his side, she turned across the track
of the moon and bounded into the wide south.
A maze of marsh islands—huddling along that
narrow, half-drowned mainland of cypress
swamp and trembling prairie which follows the
Mississippi out to sea—slept, leagues away, below the western waters. In the east lay but
one slender boundary between the voyager
and the shoreless deep, and this was so near
that from its farther edge came, now and again,
its admonishing murmur, the surf-thunder of
the open Gulf, rolling forever down the prone
but unshaken battle-front of the sandy Chan-
deleurs.

So all night, lest wind or resolve should fail
next day, he sailed. How to tell just where
dawn found him I scarcely know.

Somewhere in that blue wilderness, with no
other shore in sight, yet not over three miles
northeast of a " pass " between two long tide-

covered sand-reefs, a ferment of delta silt—if science guesses right—had lifted higher than most of the islands behind it in the sunken west one mere islet in the shape of a broad crescent, with its outward curve to seaward and a deep, slender lagoon on the landward side filling the whole length of its bay. About half the island was flat and was covered with those strong marsh grasses for which you've seen cattle, on the mainland, venture so hungrily into the deep ooze. The rest, the southern half, rose in dazzling white dunes, twenty feet or more in height, and dappled green with patches of ragged sod and thin groups of dwarfed and wind-flattened shrubs.

As the sun rose, *Sweetheart* and her sailor glided through a gap in the sand-reef that closed the lagoon in, luffed, and as a great cloud of nesting pelicans rose from their dirty town on the flats, ran softly upon the inner sands, where a rillet, a mere thread of sweet water, trickled across the white beach. Here he waded ashore with the utensils and provisions, made a fire, washed down a hot breakfast of bacon and cornbread with a pint of black coffee, returned to his boat and slept until afternoon. Wakened at length by the upturning of the sloop with the fall of the tide, he rose, rekindled his fire, cooked and ate again, smoked two pipes, and then, idly shouldering his gun, made a long half-circuit of the beach to south and east- ward, mounted the highest dune and gazed far and wide.

Nowhere on sand or sea, under the boundless dome, was there sign of human presence on the earth. Nor would there likely be any. Except by misadventure no ship on any course ever showed more than a topmast above this hori- zon. Of the hunters and fishermen who roamed the islands nearer shore . . . few knew the way hither and fewer ever sailed it. At the sound of his gun, the birds of the beach—sea-snipe, curlew, plover—showed the whites of their wings for an instant and fell to feeding again. Save when the swift *Wilderness* — you re- member the revenue cutter—chanced this way on her wide patrol, only the steamer of the lighthouse inspection service, once a month, came up out of the southwest through yonder channel and passed within hail on her way from the stations of the Belize to those of Missis- sippi Sound; and he knew—had known before he left the New Basin—that she had just gone by here the day before.

But to Gregory this solitude brought no quick distress. With a bird or two at his belt he turned again toward his dying fire. Once on the way he paused, as he came in sight of the sloop, and gazed upon it with a faintness of heart he had not known since his voyage began. However, it presently left him, and hurrying down to her side, he began to unload her completely, and to make a permanent camp in the lee of a ridge of sand crested with dwarfed casino bushes, well up from the beach. The night did not stop him, and by the time he was tired enough for sleep he had lightened the boat of everything stowed into her the previous day. Before sunrise he was at work again, removing her sandbags, her sails, flags, cordage, even her spars. The mast would have been heavy for two men to handle, but he got it out whole, though not without hurting one hand so painfully that he had to lie off for over two hours. But by mid-day he was busy again, and when at low water poor *Sweetheart* comfortably turned upon her side on the odorous, clean sand, it was never more to rise. The keen, new axe of her master ended her days.

"No! O no!" he said to me, "call it anything but courage! I felt—I felt as though I were a murderer. All I knew was that it had to be done. I trembled like a thief. I had to stoop twice before I could take up the axe, and I was so cold my teeth chattered. When I lifted the first blow I didn't know where it was going to fall. But it struck as true as a die, and then I flew at it. I never chopped so fast or clean in my life. I wasn't fierce; I was as full of self-delight as an overpraised child. And yet when something delayed me an instant, I found I was still shaking. Courage," said he, "O no; I know what it was, and I knew then. But I had no choice; it was my last chance."

I told him that any one might have thought him a madman chopping up his last chance.

"Maybe so," he replied, "but I wasn't; it was the one sane thing I could do;" and he went on to tell me, that when night fell the tallest fire that ever leapt from those sands blazed from *Sweetheart's* piled ribs and keel.

It was proof to him of his having been shrewd, he said, that for many days he felt no repentance of the act, nor was in the least lonely. There was an infinite relief merely in getting clean away from the huge world of men, with all its exactions and temptations and the myriad rebukes and rebuffs of its rude propriety and thrift. He had endured solitude enough in it. . . . Here was life begun over, with none to make new debts to except nature and himself, and no besetments but those within himself. What humble, happy masterhood! Each dawn he rose from dreamless sleep and leaped into the surf as into the embrace of a new existence. Every hour of day brought some happy task or health-giving pastime. With sheath-knife and sail-needle he made of his mainsail a handsome tent, using the mainboom for his ridge-pole, and finishing it just in time for the first night of rain—when, nevertheless, he lost all his coffee.

He did not waste toil. He hoarded its opportunities as one might treasure salt on the mountains or water in the desert, and loitering in well-calculated idleness between thoughts many and things of sea and shore innumerable, filled the intervals from labor to labor with gentle entertainment. Skyward ponderings by night, canny discoveries under foot by day, quickened his mind and sight to vast and to minute significancies, until they declared an Author known to him hitherto only by tradition. Every acre of the barren islet grew fertile in beauties and mysteries, and a handful of sand at the door of his tent held him for hours guessing the titanic battles that had ground the invincible quartz to that crystal meal and fed it to the sea.

I may be more rhetorical than he was, but

he made all the more of these conditions while experiencing them, because he knew they could not last out the thirty days, nor half the thirty, and took modest comfort in a will strong enough to meet all present demands, well knowing there was one demand yet to arise, one old usurer still to be settled with who had not yet brought in his dun.

It came—began to come—in the middle of the second week. At its familiar approach he felt no dismay, save a certain dull dismay that it brought none. Three, four, five times he went bravely to the rill, drowned his thirst and called himself satisfied; but the second day was worse than the first; the craving seemed better than the rill's brief cure of it, and once he rose straight from drinking of the stream and climbed the dune to look for a sail.

He strove in vain to labor. The pleasures of toil were as stale as those of idleness. His books were put aside with a shudder, and he walked abroad with a changed gait; the old extortioner was levying on his nerves. And on his brain. He dreamed that night of war-times; found himself commander of a whole battery of heavy guns, and lo, they were all quaker-cannon. When he would have fled, monstrous terrors met him at every turn, till he woke and could sleep no more. Dawn widened over sky and sea, but its vast beauty only mocked the castaway. All day long he wandered up and down and along and across his glittering prison, no tiniest speck of canvas, no faintest wreath of smoke, on any water's edge; the horror of his isolation growing—growing—like the monsters of his dream, and his whole nature wild with a desire which was no longer a mere physical drought, but a passion of the soul, that gave the will an unnatural energy and set at naught every true interest of earth and heaven. Again and again he would have shrieked its anguish, but the first note of his voice rebuked him to silence as if he had seen himself in a glass. He fell on his face voiceless, writhing, and promised himself, nay, pledged creation and its Creator, that on the day of his return to the walks of men he would drink the cup of madness and would drink it thenceforth till he died.

When night came again he paced the sands for hours and then fell to work to drag by long and toiling zig-zags to a favorable point on the southern end of the island the mast he had saved, and to raise there a flag of distress. In the shortness of his resources he dared not choose the most open points, where the first

high wind would cast it down; but where he
placed it it could be seen from every quarter
except the north, and any sail approaching
from that direction was sure to come within
hail even of the voice.

Day had come again as he left the finished
task, and once more from the highest wind-
built ridge his hungering eyes swept the round
sea's edge. But he saw no sail. Nerveless
and exhausted, he descended to the southeast-
ern beach and watched the morning brighten.
The breezes, that for some time had slept, fit-
fully revived, and the sun leaped from the sea
and burned its way through a low bank of dark
and ruddy clouds with so unusual a splendor,
that the beholder was, in some degree, both
quickened and calmed. He could even play at
self-command, and in child fashion bound himself not to mount the dunes again for a northern look within an hour. This southern half-
circle must suffice. Indeed, unless these idle
zephyrs should amend, no sail could in that
time draw near enough to notice any signal
he could offer.

Playing at self-command gave him some
earnest of it. In a whim of the better man he
put off his clothes and sprang into the break-
ers. He had grown chill, but a long wrestle

with the surf warmed his blood, and, as he re-
clothed himself and with a better step took his
way along the beach toward his tent, a return-
ing zest of manhood refreshed his spirit. The
hour was up, but in a kind of equilibrium of
impulses and with much emptiness of mind, he
let it lengthen on, made a fire, and, for the first
time in two days, cooked food. He ate and
still tarried.

A brand in his camp fire, a piece from the
remnant of his boat, made beautiful flames.
He idly cast in another and was pleased to
find himself sitting there instead of gazing
his eyes out for sails that never rose into
view. He watched a third brand smoke and
blaze. And then, as tamely as if the new impulse were only another part of a continued
abstraction, he arose and once more climbed
the sandy hills.

The highest was some distance from his
camp. At one point near its top a brief
northeastward glimpse of the marsh's outer
edge and the blue waters beyond showed at
least that nothing had come near enough to
raise the pelicans. But the instant his sight
cleared the crown of the ridge, he rushed forward, threw up his arms, and lifted his voice
in a long, imploring yell. Hardly two miles

away, her shapely canvas leaning and stiffen-
ing in the augmented breeze, a small yacht had
just gone about, and with twice the speed at
which she must have approached was hurrying back straight into the north.

The frantic man dashed back and forth
along the crest, tossing his arms, waving his
Madras handkerchief, cursing himself for leaving his gun so far behind, and again and again
repeating his vain ahoys in wilder and wilder
alternations of beseeching and rage. The less-
ening craft flew straight on, no ear in her
skilled enough to catch the distant cry, and no
eye alert enough to scan the dwindling sandhills. He ceased to call, but still, with heavy
notes of distress to himself, waved and waved,
now here, now there, while the sail grew
smaller and smaller.

At length he stopped this also and only
stood gazing. Almost on first sight of the
craft he had guessed that the men in her
had taken alarm at the signs of changing
weather, and seeing the freshening smoke of
his fire had also inferred that earlier sports-
men were already on the island. Oh, if he
could have fired one shot when she was nearest! But already she was as hopelessly gone
as though she were even now below the ho-

rizon. Suddenly he turned and ran down to his camp. Not for the gun; not in any new hope of signaling the yacht. No, no; a raft! a raft! Deliverance or destruction, it should be at his own hand and should wait no longer!

A raft forthwith he set about to make. Some stout portions of his boat were still left. Tough shrubs of the sandhills furnished trennels and suppler parts. Of ropes there was no lack. The mast was easily dragged down again to the beach to be once more a mast, and in nervous haste, yet with skill and thoroughness, the tent was ripped up and remade into a sail, and even a rude centreboard was rigged in order that one might tack against unfavorable winds.

Winds, at nightfall, when the thing began to be near completion, there were none. The day's sky had steadily withdrawn its favor. The sun shone as it sank into the waves, but in the northwest and southeast, dazzling thunderheads swelled from the sea's line high into the heavens, and in the early dusk began, with silent kindlings, to challenge each other to battle. As night swiftly closed down the air grew unnaturally still. From the toiler's brow, worse than at noon, the sweat rolled off, as at last he brought his work to a close by the glare of his

leaping camp-fire. Now, unless he meant only
to perish, he must once more eat and sleep
while he might. Then let the storm fall; the
moment it was safely over and the wind in the
right quarter he would sail. As for the thirst
which had been such torture while thwarted,
now that it ruled unchallenged, it was purely
a wild, glad zeal, as full of method as of dili-
gence. But first he must make his diminished
provisions and his powder safe against the
weather; and this he did, covering them with
a waterproof stuff and burying them in a
northern slope of sand.

He awoke in the small hours of the night.
The stars of the zenith were quenched. Blackness walled and roofed him in close about his
crumbled fire, save when at shorter and shorter
intervals and with more and more deafening
thunders the huge clouds lit up their own
forms writhing one upon another, and revealed
the awe-struck sea and ghostly sands waiting
breathlessly below. He rose to lay on more
fuel, and while he was in the act the tornado
broke upon him. The wind, as he had fore-
cast, came out of the southeast. In an instant
it was roaring and hurtling against the farther
side of his island rampart like the charge of a
hundred thousand horse and tossing the sand

of the dunes like blown hair into the northwest, while the rain, in one wild deluge, lashed the frantic sea and weltering lagoon as with the whips of the Furies.

He had kept the sail on the beach for a protection from the storm, but before he could crawl under it he was as wet as though he had been tossed up by the deep, and yet was glad to gain its cover from the blinding floods and stinging sand. Here he lay for more than an hour, the rage of the tempest continually growing, the heavens in a constant pulsing glare of lightnings, their terrific thunders smiting and bellowing round and round its echoing vault, and the very island seeming at times to stagger back and recover again as it braced itself against the fearful onsets of the wind. Snuggling in his sail-cloth burrow, he complacently recalled an earlier storm like this, which he and *Sweetheart*, the only other time they ever were here, had calmly weathered in this same lagoon. On the mainland, in that storm, cane- and rice-fields had been laid low and half destroyed, houses had been unroofed, men had been killed. A woman and a boy, under a pecan-tree, were struck by lightning ; and three men who had covered themselves with a tarpaulin on one of the wharves in New Orleans were blown with it into the Mississippi, poor fellows, and were drowned; a fact worthy of second consideration in the present case.

This second thought had hardly been given it before he crept hastily from his refuge and faced the gale in quick alarm. The hurricane was veering to southward. Let it shift but a point or two more, and its entire force would sweep the lagoon and its beach. Before long the change came. The mass of canvas at his feet leaped clear of the ground and fell two or three yards away. He sprang to seize it, but in the same instant the whole storm—rain, wind, and sand—whirled like a troop of fiends round the southern end of the island, the ceaseless lightnings showing the way, and came tearing and howling up its hither side. The white sail lifted, bellied, rolled, fell, vaulted into the air, fell again, tumbled on, and at the foot of a dune stopped, until its wind-buffeted pursuer had almost overtaken it. Then it fled again, faster, faster, higher, higher up the sandy slope to its top, caught and clung an instant on some unseen bush, and then with one mad bound into the black sky, unrolled, widened like a phantom, and vanished forever.

Gregory turned in desperation, and in the

glare of the lightning, looked back toward his raft. Great waves were rolling along and across the slender reef in wide obliques and beating themselves to death in the lagoon, or sweeping out of it again seaward at its more northern end. On the dishevelled crest of one he saw his raft, and on another its mast. He could not look a second time. The flying sand blinded him and cut the blood from his face. He could only cover his eyes and crawl under the bushes in such poor lee as he could find; and there, with the first lull of the storm, heavy with exhaustion and despair, he fell asleep and slept until far into the day. When he awoke the tempest was over.

Even more completely the tumult within him was quieted. He rose and stood forth mute in spirit as in speech; humbled, yet content, in the consciousness that having miserably failed, first to save himself, and then to rue himself back to destruction, the hurricane had been his deliverer. It had spared his supplies, his ammunition, his weapons, only hiding them deeper under the dune sands; but scarce a vestige of his camp remained and of his raft nothing. As once more from the highest sandridge he looked down upon the sea weltering in the majestic after-heavings of its passion,

at the eastern beach booming under the shock
of its lofty rollers, and then into the sky still
gray with the endless flight of southward-
hurrying scud, he felt the stir of a new attach-
ment to them and his wild prison, and pledged
alliance with them thenceforth.

Here, in giving me his account, Gregory
asked me if that sounded sentimental. I said
no, and thereupon he actually tried to apolo-
gize to me as though I were a professional
story-teller, for having had so few deep feelings
in the moments where the romancists are supposed to place them. I told him what I had
once seen a mechanic do on a steep, slated roof
nearly a hundred feet from the pavement. He
had faced around from his work, which was
close to the ridge-tiles, probably to kick off the
shabby shoes he had on, when some hold failed
him and he began to slide toward the eaves.
We people in the street below fairly moaned
our horror, but he didn't utter a sound. He
held back with all his skill, one leg thrust out
in front, the other drawn up with the knee to
his breast, and his hands flattened beside him
on the slates, but he came steadily on down
till his forward foot passed over the eaves and
his heel caught on the tin gutter. Then he
stopped. We held our breath below. He

slowly and cautiously threw off one shoe, then the other, and then turned, climbed back up the roof and resumed his work. And we two or three witnesses down in the street didn't think any less of him because he did so without any show of our glad emotion.

"O, if I'd had that fellow's nerve," said Gregory, "that would be another thing!"

My wife and I smiled at each other.

"How would it be 'another thing?'" we asked. "Did *you* not quietly get up and begin life over again as if nothing had occurred?"

"There wasn't anything else to do," he replied, with a smile. "The feelings came later, too, in an easy sort o' gradual way. I never could quite make out how men get such clear notions of what they call 'Providence,' but, just the same, I know by experience there's all the difference of peace and misery, or life and death, whether you're in partnership with the things that help the world on, or with those that hold it back."

"But with that feeling," my wife asked, "did not your longing for our human world continue?"

"No," he replied, "but I got a new liking for it—although, you understand, *I* never had anything against *it*, of course. It's too big and

strong for me, that's all; and that's my fault.
Your man on that slippery roof, kicking his
shoes off, is a sort of parable to me. If your
hand or your foot offend you and you have
to cut it off, that's a physical disablement, and
bad enough. But when your gloves and your
shoes are too much for you, and you have to
pluck *them* off and cast them from you, you
find each one is a great big piece of the civilized
world, and you hardly know how much you
did like it, till you've lost it. And still, it's no
use longing, when you know your limitations,
and I saw I'd got to keep *my* world trimmed
down to where I could run barefooted on the
sand."

He told us that now he began, for the first
time since coming to the island, to find his
books his best source of interest and diversion.
He learned, he said, a way of reading by which
sea, sky, book, island, and absent humanity, all
seemed parts of one whole, and all to speak
together in one harmony, while they toiled
together for one harmony, some day to be per-
fected. Not all books, nor even all good books,
were equally good for that effect, he thought,
and the best——

" You might not think it," he said, " but the
best was a Bible I'd chanced to carry along ; "

he didn't know precisely what kind, but "just one of these ordinary Bibles you see lying around in people's houses." He extolled the psalms and asked my wife if she'd ever noticed the beauty of the twenty-third. She smiled and said she believed she had.

"Then there was one," he went on, "beginning, 'Lord, my heart is not haughty, nor mine eyes lofty; neither do I exercise myself in great matters, or in things too wonderful for me;' and by and by, it says, 'Surely, I have quieted myself as a child that is weaned: my soul is even as a weaned child.' "

One day, after a most marvellous sunset, he had been reading, he said, "that long psalm with twenty-two parts in it—a hundred and seventy-six verses." He had intended to read "Lord, my heart is not haughty" after it, though the light was fast failing, but at the hundred and seventy-sixth verse, he closed the book. Thus he sat in the nearly motionless air, gazing on the ripples of the lagoon as, now singly, and now by twos or threes, they glided up the beach, tinged with the colors of parting day as with a grace of resignation, and sank into the grateful sands like the lines of this last verse sinking into his heart; now singly—"I have gone astray like a lost sheep;" and now

by twos—"I have gone astray like a lost
sheep; save thy servant;" or by threes—"I
have gone astray like a lost sheep; save thy
servant; for I do not forget thy command-
ments."

"I shouldn't tell that," he said to us, "if I
didn't know so well how little it counts for.
But I knew at the time that when the next day
but one should bring the light-house steamer, I
shouldn't be any more fit to go ashore, *to stay*,
than a jelly-fish." We agreed, he and I, that
there can be as wide a distance between fine
feelings and faithful doing as, he said, "between listening to the band, and charging a
battery."

On the islet the night deepened. The moon
had not risen, and the stars only glorified the
dark, as it, in turn, revealed the unearthly
beauties of a phosphorescent sea. It was one
of those rare hours in which the deep confessed the amazing numbers of its own living
and swarming constellations. Not a fish could
leap or dart, not a sinuous thing could turn, but
it became an animate torch. Every quick movement was a gleam of green fire. No drifting
life could pulse so softly along but it betrayed
itself in lambent outlines. Each throb of the
water became a beam of light, and every ripple

that widened over the strand—still whispering,
" I have gone astray "—was edged with lumi-
nous pearls.

In an agreeable weariness of frame, un-
troubled in mind, and counting the night too
beautiful for slumber, he reclined on the dry
sands with an arm thrown over a small pile of
fagots which he had spent the day in gathering
from every part of the island to serve his need
for the brief remainder of his stay. In this
search he had found but one piece of his boat,
a pine board. This he had been glad to rive
into long splinters and bind together again as
a brand, with which to signal the steamer if—
contrary to her practice, I think he said—she
should pass in the night. And so, without a pre-
monition of drowsiness, he was presently asleep,
with the hours radiantly folding and expiring
one upon another like the ripples on the beach.

When he came to himself he was on his feet.
The moon was high, his fire was smouldering ;
his heart was beating madly and his eyes were
fixed on the steamer, looming large, moving at
full speed, her green light showing, her red
light hid, and her long wake glowing with
comet fire. In a moment she would be passing.
It was too late for beacon-flame or torch. He
sprang for his gun, and, mounting the first low

rise, fired into the air, once!—twice!—and shouted, "Help!—help!"

She kept straight on. She was passing, she was passing! In trembling haste he loaded and fired again, again wailed out his cry for help, and still she kept her speed. He had loaded for the third discharge, still frantically calling the while, and was lifting his gun to fire when he saw the white light at her foremast head begin to draw nearer to the green light at her waist and knew she was turning. He fired, shouted, and tried to load again; but as her red light brightened into view beside the green, he dropped his gun and leaped and crouched and laughed and wept for joy.

"Why, Gregory!" the naval lieutenant cried, as the castaway climbed from the steamer's boat to her deck. "Why, you blasted old cracked fiddle! what in——"

"Right, the first guess!" laughed Gregory, "there's where I've been!" and in the cabin he explained all.

"The fiddle's mended," he concluded. "You can play a tune on it—by being careful."

"But what's your tune?" asked his hearer; "you cannot go back to that island."

"Yes, I'll be on it in a week—with a schooner-load of cattle. I can get them on credit. Going to raise cattle there as a regular business. They'll fatten in that marsh like blackbirds."

True enough, before the week was up the mended fiddle was playing its tune. It was not until Gregory's second return from his island that he came to see us and told us his simple story. We asked him how it was that the steamer, that first time, had come so much earlier than she generally did.

"She didn't," he replied. "I had miscount- ed one day."

"Don't you," asked my wife, who would have liked a more religious tone in Gregory's recital, "don't you have trouble to keep run of your Sabbaths away out there alone?"

"Why"—he smiled—"it's always Sunday there. Here almost everybody feels duty bound to work harder than somebody else, or else make somebody else work harder than he, and you need a day every now and then for Sunday—or Sabbath, at least. Oh, I sup- pose it's all one in the end, isn't it? You take your's in a pill, I take mine in a powder. Not that it's the least bit like a dose, however, ex- cept for the good it does."

"And you're really prospering, even in a material way!" I said.

"Yes," he answered. "O yes; the island's already too small for us."

"It's certainly very dangerously exposed," said my wife, and I guessed her thought was on Last Island, which, you remember, though very large and populous, had been, within our recollection, totally submerged, with dreadful loss of life.

"O yes," he responded, "there's always something, wherever you are. One of these days some storm's going to roll the sea clean over the whole thing."

"Then, why don't you move to a bigger island closer inshore?" she asked.

"I'm afraid," said Gregory, and smiled.

"Afraid!" said my wife, incredulously.

"Yes," he responded. "I'm afraid my prisoner'll get away from me."

As his hand closed over hers in good-by, I saw, what he could not, that she had half a notion to kiss it. I told her so when he was gone, and kissed hers—for him.

"I don't care," she said, dreamily, as it lingered in mine, "I'm glad I mended his coat for him that time."

"SPRING warmth, blossoming of flowers, dif-
fusion of sunlight,—that would be the true interpretation of your father," some one has said
to me.   Yes, all that and more—the nourishing
of all things good and beautiful.   The tender
care of frail and delicate life, the protection of
weakness from the cold blasts of the harsh,
wintry world.   Mr. Barrie, in his introduction
to the British edition of the *Grandissimes*,
says: "I like him best when his one arm pro-
tects some poor, wounded quadroon, and he is
fighting for her with the other."   It is this, I
think, that is the key-note to the man.   Witty,
vivacious, merry, teeming with restless energy
he may be and almost constantly is; yet beneath all this is a tenderness, a passionate sympathy for the "under side," a great-heartedness
that makes him what he is, a true poet and a
lover of all mankind—and, better still, a noble
man.

This sympathy for the "under side" is not a
mere sentiment with him—it is that truest of

all sympathy that comes from a heart that has itself known the under side of life. From his early youth he struggled face to face with hardship—even in his boyhood he knew what it meant to fight for a living, and to work not only for his own bread but for that of his mother and sisters. "Our life," says my father's eldest sister, "was a very quiet one and quite without incident." This was the one chief incident: that, in his fifteenth year, his father suddenly died, leaving the support of the family almost entirely to the care of himself and this sister; naturally there was very little time left for other incidents.

Yet this was doubtless a blessing in disguise, for his own hard work roused in him a kindred feeling for all who labor and are heavy laden; and this feeling, with the knowledge of the inner nature of toil and poverty, strengthened a deep desire to make right triumph and the strong protect the weak.

Some have thought it strange, indeed, that he should so valiantly defend the rights of the negro as he conceived them, though he was born in New Orleans and lived there for the first forty years of his life; was himself the son and grandson of slave-owners and served in the Confederate army through the Civil War. How is it

11

strange? He was a mere boy when the war broke out, and nothing could have been more natural than that he should fight with all a boy's enthusiasm and loyalty for his native place and for the traditions of his family. Afterward he looked at it with a larger vision and a clearer discrimination and knew that he could no longer accept the theories for which he had once stood so bravely. And because he *was* a Southerner and had lived among slave-owners, he saw far better than any stranger could have seen, the terrible suffering, the cruelties, the barbarities inflicted upon the negro slaves, and his ever-ready sympathy for the oppressed, his bitter scorn for all oppres- sion, flashed forth as an inevitable result.

No story of his shows this more clearly than that of Bras-Coupé, that king and great soldier among his own black men, that slave and half-beast among white men. Under the barbarous cruelties that were put upon him, his indomit-able self-will, his invincible courage, his fiery spirit reigned supreme, and he died a hero, the admiration of his tormentors. But, as my father himself has said to me, "Behind all these facts and incidents, I was deeply stirred to make a story of them by the very natural re-volt of feeling I experienced about this time in becoming acquainted with the harsher provisions of the old Black Code of Louisiana."

This love for suffering humanity, this intense hatred for all tyranny of strength over weakness, of evil over good, is one of the deepest inlaid characteristics of his nature. As a child, his tenderest care and solicitude were for the weaklings, the helpless creatures in his little world; his tiny plants were nourished most lovingly, and on his daily walks with his younger brother he would, oftener than not, bring home a wounded bird or a motherless chicken, cherished in his warm, protecting hand. In our home in New Orleans, too, I remember how often he would return from his rambles with some hurt, helpless little creature of the fields or woods, until there were so many that a room was specially fitted up for them in the basement of the house.

Perhaps you will think, as many, I know, do think, that with sentiments so widely different from those of the people among whom he was brought up, he could have nothing in harmony with them or with the South. But, indeed, he is no alien child of the South. The very atmosphere of New Orleans, with its bright, sunny warmth, its wealth of color, its luxuriance of heavily-scented flowers, is an integral part of his nature; his eager love for the artistic, his keen appreciation of the picturesque, of all that is of the Old World, quaint and indolently charming, as opposed to the glaringly modern and unlovely side of the New World—all this is as strong in his heart as it ever was in a Grandissime of the Grandissimes. But, on the other side, and almost as distinct as if he were two men in one, are those characteristics which he inherited from his Northern mother—an intense energy, an eager, far-reaching ambition, a vivacity like that of quicksilver, always restless, incessantly doing, doing. He has always seemed to me the epitome of energy—untiring. alert, unswerving in purpose, a single day's holiday seems to him time uselessly spent. These qualities, together with a keen, penetrating insight, have made him quick to see and understand wrong wherever it lay, and to bend all his strength toward righting it.

He has never looked on the dark side of life with any pessimism; his nature is too sunny— it leaves very few dark shadows. One of his literary friends once said of him, " Cable could never create a villain;" and whether he could or not, he never has. His search has ever been for the good, the true, and the beautiful, for the artistic, for the picturesque. When a young man, living in New Orleans, the quaint beauty, the picturesque Old-World fashions and customs of the Creole life appealed to him strongly, and he then made the careful study of that odd little world and of some of its conspicuous characters which enabled him later to write his Creole stories.

These stories of Creole life are what he is known by chiefly to-day, but they were not his first literary work. His earliest writing was done as a reporter on the New Orleans *Picayune*, and it was not long after he began filling a weekly column in that paper that the attention of the New Orleans public was attracted to him. He tells an amusing story about a little poem written for this column—one which has since become more widely known as almost the only bit of verse he has ever written. This was inspired by the birth of his eldest child, as also by the knowledge that his column for the paper was still incomplete on the night before it was due. Lack of sleep and a certain nervousness due to the event had taxed his ingenuity and had left him somewhat at a loss as to a theme for his weekly writing. Nevertheless he rose to the occasion and wrote the following verses in a few moments of delightful inspiration :

THE NEW ARRIVAL

There came to port last Sunday night
  The queerest little craft,
Without an inch of rigging on ;
  I looked and looked and laughed.
It seemed so curious that she
  Should cross the Unknown water,
And moor herself right in my room,
  My daughter, O my daughter !

Yet by these presents witness all
  She's welcome fifty times,
And comes consigned to Hope and Love
  And common-metre rhymes.
She has no manifest but this,
  No flag floats o'er the water,
She's too new for the British Lloyds—
  My daughter, O my daughter !

Ring out wild bells, and tame ones too !
  Ring out the lovers' moon !
Ring in the little worsted socks !
  Ring in the bib and spoon !
Ring out the muse ! ring in the nurse !
  Ring in the milk and water !
Away with paper, pen and ink—
  My daughter, O my daughter !

These verses were a decided success at the
time, and have since appeared in various parts
of the country, claiming a different authorship

each time. They are slight perhaps in themselves, but full of the overflowing tenderness,
the merry humor, the great, yet childlike heart,
that are his strongest characteristics—the childlike heart that with children is always merry,
bright, tenderly sympathetic, yet deeply serious. Closely akin to this little poem are the
following letters written to his eldest children:

NEW ORLEANS, September 2, 1875.
MISSES LOUISE AND MARY AND
    MASTER GEORGE B. CABLE.
DEAR LADIES AND SIR:—It gives me great pleasure
to write to you, and I make haste to thank Miss Louise and
Miss Mary for their gracefully written and really eloquent
letters to me. When I hear that you are enjoying the
pleasures of the sea-side, I am so delighted that I open
my sleeve slyly and laugh right into it till it is as full
of laugh as a bath-house. I have a hole in the elbow for
this very purpose. A man named *Pauvreté* (Poverty), a
Frenchman, made it for me for nothing. Some of these
days I hope to come and take tea with you in your tea-set;
that is if it lasts long enough. But if not I suppose we can
have a new tea-set made; they make them in Germany.
I'll try and have the money to pay for them.

I must tell you that I have bought a big doll for myself.
It is only a head, to be sure, but it is as big as a water-
melon and is named Cicero. You'll see it when we all get
home. God speed the day.

Your loving father,
G. W. CABLE.

UNION CLUB, BOSTON, June 10, 1881.

MY DEAR LITTLE DAUGHTER :—I must send you a line for your own dear self.   I am anxious to hear from you as well as from sweet mother, and I hope I may get a word or two from your own hand.

I could not in a whole hour tell you all the things I have seen since we parted.   But I can say that all the time I saw the beauties of land or sea or hill or valley, whether nature's work or man's, I was still thinking of my beloved ones far away on the mountains.

Yet I did not fret, for I know that the Good Shepherd keeps my little flock, and my prayer is that their souls may be precious in His sight.   I pray that they may be sweet, gentle, obedient children, trying to do their parents' will before the parents have to express it.

Be careful to help each other.   Be amiable each to each. Remember in everything you do you are serving God.   Do everything cheerfully—gladly.

Tell Mary not to tease and to keep her face at least half clean.

Tell Lucy I wish I had her here now with a little salt and pepper and mustard.   I would eat her for dinner.

Tell Margaret not to forget her breakfast in the morning, her dinner afterwards, nor her supper in the evening. Tell her not to be cross to Lucy and to mind mother as well as sister Louise.

Now, form in procession and each kiss mother as you pass by.

Here are four kisses for four sweet girls and four for their dear mother.

Your affectionate father,

G. W. CABLE.

NEW YORK, October 16, 1882.

My Two Darling Little Honey-Bees: — I shall have to write to you both at once, as I believe I have not yet answered Louise's letter.

It makes me very happy to have such good accounts of you, both from mother and Aunt Mary.

You are my precious treasures. Everybody remembers, here, how nicely you took care of yourselves and of one another when you were in New York last year.

I am pleased with the school-paper idea. Your circulation is small, I suppose, but select. The Century prints this month, 140,000 copies.

I want each of you to kiss Margaret and Lucy for me.

I will give you some items for your paper. Let me see :

1. Mr. Joseph Pennell, the noted artist and etcher, will leave America for Europe about the 1st of next January, to make sketches of Italian architecture.

2. Oriental rugs are being imported to New York and freely sold. A fine eastern rug is more beautiful after it has been used for a hundred years than it was when it was new. Some are made of wool and some of silk.

Kiss the dear, dear mother.

Your affectionate father,

G. W. CABLE.

3. Mr. Charles Dudley Warner has returned to America.

My father is ranked among the Southern writers of to-day, both as a Southerner himself and as a portrayer of Southern life, and many do not hesitate to give him there, the highest place. He is, among prose writers, as Matthew

Arnold among poets, one to be truly appre-
ciated most by those who love purity of form,
delicacy of expression, exquisite grace and
beauty of tone; although he has also the
power of giving us that which is vital in
feeling. He is far too painstaking to gratify
an omniverous taste. He writes slowly and
carefully, considering every word and polish-
ing every sentence, but for this very reason
his work will live. He is patient always to
work long and hard, if in the end he shall
have obtained his purpose—truth, reality, the
absence of any false note, in word or tone;
and patient not only with himself but with
others who work slowly, but steadily on. Not
long ago, a class of little boys each wrote
him a Christmas letter to show their appreciation of certain of his stories which they
had been reading in school; he replied in one
letter to the whole class. But there was one
boy who had been left out because he was
too slow; he had taken great care to illumi-
nate and illustrate his letter and it was not
finished in time to be sent with the others.
He was guyed by his little friends, called
"slow-boy," and told that he was "left" because of his slowness. But the older "slow-
boy," when he heard the story, showed imme-

diate sympathy with the little boy who took pains and who slowly and carefully worked out his own purpose, and he wrote him this letter, for himself alone, thus delighting the boy and saving his reputation among his schoolmates.

DEAR S——:

I want that letter you wrote for my Christmas. Maybe you have destroyed it. If so, never mind, we are friends anyhow. And all the more are we friends because we don't generally get things done as quickly as some other people, very able and delightful people, too, can do them.

My main purpose in writing this is to thank you for your intention, and to say that I regret your name was not in the list of those to whom I replied.

Yours truly,
GEORGE W. CABLE.

He has now lived for almost fifteen years in the North, but more than half of his work was done while he lived in New Orleans, and it is to the South he still turns as to his real home and his true source of inspiration. He left New Orleans, not because he had grown out of sympathy with the South, or had ceased to love it, nor because, as some have thought, he was driven from it by the enmity of the Southerners, but because he felt the disadvantage in so one-sided a view of the people of whom he wrote. This, and more private reasons, brought him to make his home in the North, and here at " Tarryawhile " he finally settled, nearly seven years ago.

This house is on the edge of a beautiful strip of woods, where he loves to wander daily, where he knows every tree and shrub by name and has at least a " speaking acquaintance " with every bird. To the forest trees he has added, from time to time, other trees, planted as memorials of happy days with various guests. The latest additions to the ranks are a tulip-tree, planted by Mr. Franklin Head, of Chicago, and a horse-chestnut, planted on the same day, with the assistance of Mrs. Wynne, as a page in our guest-book bears witness.

Franklin H. Head, September 22, 1898.

TREE-PLANTING DAY.

" O friends whose hearts still hold their prime,
   Whose bright example warms and cheers,
  You teach us how to smile at Time
   And set to music all his years."

Let the tree speak for me in the coming years.
                    MADELENE YALE WYNNE.

In this same guest-book is another inscription bearing the date on which Mr. Barrie

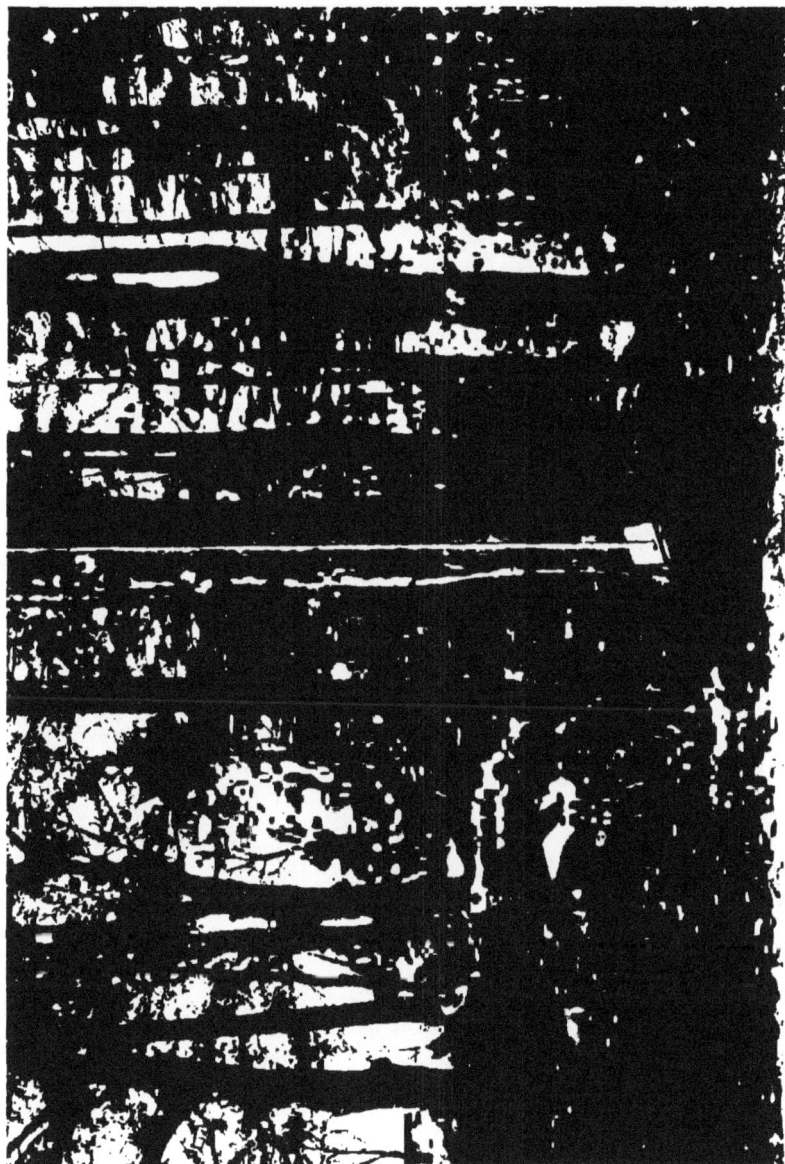

THE SWING WALK, TARRYAWHILE.

planted a tree. The quotation in the book is this:

" Intelligence and courtesy not always are combined,
Often in a wooden house, a golden room we find."

And beneath this is written:

If you would find this golden room, take the train to Northampton, Mass., go up Elm Street, turn into Dryads' Green, house right-hand corner, enter, go up stairs and take the last door on the left. A golden room—a golden memory.

J. M. BARRIE,
MARY BARRIE.

October 13, 1896.

In the summer of 1898, my father left America, to be in turn the guest of Mr. Barrie in London. His trip was a short one, but Mr. Barrie's "golden memory" could scarcely bear half so bright a lustre as does that which still lingers with his guest. It was his first visit to England, his first introduction into the literary circles of England and Scotland, and his impressions, as he has written them fully in a diary kept at the time, have a bright halo around them—"a light that never was on land or sea."

The impression he left behind was not wholly unpleasant either, as several have testified. When some one wrote to Mr. Andrew Carnegie,

speaking of my father's visit with him at Skibo
Castle, he sent this in reply :—

With some experience, but not as much as desired, to
justify an opinion, we pronounce Mr. Cable the most delightful of visitors.   Every day some new charm is found
in him.   He glides into the bosom of the family before
we are aware, without effort, and becomes one of us.   He
carries an atmosphere with him which gently and insensibly
envelopes the household.

But the greatest charm of all was revealed when he gave
Skibo Castle inmates a reading, for which the large hall
was admirably adapted.   Altogether fine as the performance
was, the most striking feature was this slender little delicate
writer of books, revealing himself as an actor of great
dramatic force.   For an hour he held us all spellbound.

There is, however, one serious fault with this wonderful
man, his visits are too short; although this has another
side.   He could not stay very long before we should become so dependent upon his presence as to feel his absence
too severely.   Better not get too well acquainted with him.

Was it any wonder that when he mounted the coach that
morning and waved " good-by," the feelings of the assembled household found expression in that most appropriate
of Scotch songs :

> " Better lo'ed ye canna be,
>   Will ye no come back again ? "

This "greatest charm of all "—his wonderful,
dramatic power—is a source of surprise to all
who experience it for the first time.   To his
capacity for feeling intensely the real life, the

true living quality of his own creation, is added the ability to make this life quite as intensely real in the minds of his hearers, the ability of a genuine actor; surprising, in that such remarkable power should come from so slight, almost delicate, a man, and that a voice, which is one of the lowest in conversation, should display such richness of tone, such depth of feeling, such magnitude and range of expression. On one of his reading tours a number of years ago, he gave a reading in an old Puritan town of Massachusetts. The reception of his dramatic power was apparently far different from that which Mr. Carnegie describes, but it was only apparently, for the next morning he received this card :—

DEAR MR. CABLE:

In justice to your audience of this evening, we think you should be told that the people of the old Puritan town of D—— are still under the grim influence of Salem witchcraft and persecution of Quakers. Laughter still seems to them a little immoral and applause something to be indulged in with extreme moderation. Could you have heard the comments of the occupants of that horse-car mentioned by you at the introduction of your story, you would have learned how deep an impression your reading had made. As for us, we are not D—— people, and we laughed, wept and applauded as we chose. No, we laughed and wept as you chose, and applauded as we chose.

And now, we thank you for one of the great pleasures of our lives. We are not autograph hunters and so simply sign ourselves,   TWO OF THE AUDIENCE.

My father's own theory that genius does not excuse a man from his duty to family and society, is fully exemplified in his case, for with him theory is ever synonymous with practice. Carlyle was known, even by his mother, to be "gey ill to live with," but Macaulay considered it absolutely immoral that a man should be less interesting, genial and kind at home than in society, and it is surely Macaulay's example that he follows. "You are so accustomed to his wit," said a friend of his to me, "that you take it as daily food and do not know that you are being fed on nectar and ambrosia." And, indeed, it flows as freely among his family as it ever does among his outside friends or among strangers — perhaps more freely. "Did ever anyone have such a father as ours?" says one of his children, and the question is constantly echoed—but less as a question than as an unanswerable assertion—by each one of his large family.

LUCY LEFFINGWELL CABLE.
TARRYAWHILE, NORTHAMPTON,
        March, 1899.

www.ingramcontent.com/pod-product-compliance
Lightning Source LLC
Chambersburg PA
CBHW030840270326
41928CB00007B/1148